GCSE

Questions and Answers

Q&A

MATHEMATICS

KEY STAGE 4

Mark Patmore Principal Examiner
Brian Seager Chief Examiner

SERIES EDITOR: BOB McDUELL

Letts
EDUCATIONAL

Contents

HOW TO USE THIS BOOK

The purpose of the *Questions and Answers* series is to help you achieve the grades you want in your GCSEs. This book is designed to help all students aiming for grades up to and including grade B and also provides a good basis for revision for the Standard Grade of the Scottish Certificate of Education, General Level. If you are aiming for a grade A or A* at GCSE, you will find additional questions focused specifically on this area in *Letts GCSE Questions and Answers Mathematics to A**.

This book is based on the idea that an experienced Examiner can give, through exam questions, sample answers and advice, the help you need to secure success. Many revision aids concentrate on providing the facts which might have to be remembered in an exam. This book focuses on giving you invaluable practice at doing exam questions, so that you can learn to improve your exam technique.

The *Questions and Answers* series is designed to provide:

- Easy to use **Revision Summaries** which identify the important facts. These are to remind you, in summary form, of the topics you will need to have revised in order to answer exam questions. (Answers to the illustrative examples are also provided.)
- Advice on the different types of question in each subject and how to answer them well to obtain the highest marks.
- Many examples of **exam questions**, with spaces for you to fill in your answers, just as in an exam. It is best if you try the questions first before going to the answers and the advice which accompanies them. The questions are either official Exam Board questions or have been specially written by experienced Examiners who write questions for the Exam Boards.
- **Sample answers** to all of the questions.
- **Examiner's tips.** By using the experience of Examiners we are able to give advice on how your answers can be improved, and how common mistakes can be avoided.

THE IMPORTANCE OF USING QUESTIONS FOR REVISION

Past exam questions play an important part in revising for exams. However, it is important not to start practising questions too early. Nothing can be more disheartening than trying to do a question that you do not understand because you have not mastered the concepts. Therefore it is important to have studied a topic thoroughly before attempting questions on it.

It is unlikely that any question you try will appear in exactly the same form on the papers you are going to take. However the number of totally original questions that can be set on any part of the syllabus is limited and so similar ideas occur over and over again. It certainly will help you if the question you are trying to answer in an exam is familiar and you are used to the type of language used. Your confidence will be boosted, and confidence is important for exam success.

Practising exam questions will also highlight gaps in your knowledge and understanding that you can go back and revise more thoroughly.

Finally, having access to answers, as you do in this book, will enable you to see clearly what is required by the Examiner, how best to answer each question and the amount of detail required.

MAXIMISING YOUR MARKS IN MATHEMATICS

One of the keys to exam success is to know how marks are gained or lost and the Examiner's tips given with the solutions in this book give hints on how you can maximise your marks on particular questions. However, you should also take careful note of these general points:

- Check the requirements of your exam board and follow the instructions (or 'rubric') carefully. Many mathematics papers start with short, straightforward questions. You should work through them in order, so that you build up your confidence. Do not overlook any parts of a question – double-check that you have seen everything, including any questions on the back page! Take time to read through all the questions carefully, and then start with the question you think you can do best.

- Get into the habit of setting out your work neatly and logically. If you are untidy and disorganised you could penalise yourself by misreading your own figures or lose marks because your method is not obvious. Always show all necessary working so that you can obtain marks for a correct method even if your final answer is wrong. Remember that a good clear sketch can help you to see important details.
- When the question asks for a particular result to be established, remember that to obtain the method marks you must show sufficient working to convince the Examiner that your argument is valid.
- Do rough estimates of calculations to make sure that they are reasonable, state units if applicable and give answers to the required degree of accuracy; do not approximate too early in your working.
- Make sure that you are familiar with the formulae at the front of the exam paper and learn any useful formulae that are not included.
- When about 15 minutes remain, check whether you are running short of time. If so, try to score as many marks as possible in the short time that remains, concentrating on the easier parts of any questions not yet tackled.
- The following glossary may help you in answering questions:
  Write down, state – no explanation is needed for an answer.
  Calculate, find, show, solve – include enough working to make your method clear.
  Draw – plot accurately, using graph paper and selecting a suitable scale; this is usually preparation for reading information from the graph.

DIFFERENT TYPES OF EXAM QUESTION

There are different types of question which appear on exam papers. Questions on mathematics papers are of three types:

'Pure' mathematics questions

These are usually short and are focused on one particular skill or part of the syllabus.

Example 1: Solve the equation $2x - 3 = 42 - 3x$.

Answer ______________________ (2)

Structured questions

These are the most common type of question in GCSE Mathematics papers and thus most of the questions in this book are structured questions. These questions usually have a context – that is they are about the application of mathematics to a real (or nearly real!) situation.

In a structured question, the question is divided into parts (a), (b), (c) etc. These parts may be further subdivided into (i), (ii) and so on. A structure is built into the question and, hence, into your answer. Frequently, answers from one part of a question are used in subsequent parts, but an error in, say, part (a), which may result in few, or even no, marks being obtained for that part, should not result in no marks being obtained in subsequent parts, provided the incorrect answer is used 'correctly'. There are numbers in brackets, e.g. (3), to show how many marks are allocated to the various parts of a question.

Example 2: The diagram shows the design for a company's logo which is to be painted on the side of a building.

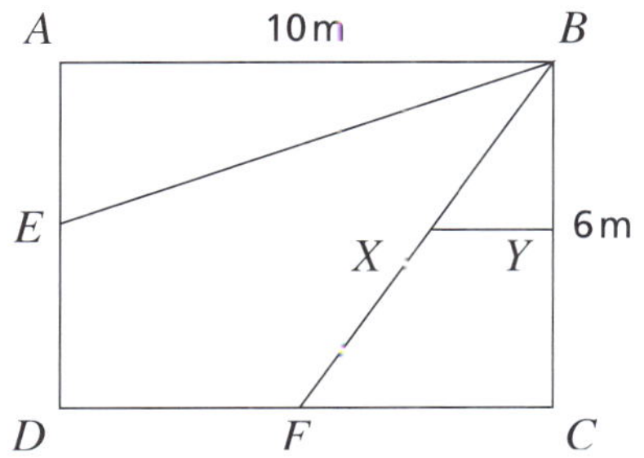

The design is a rectangle, $ABCD$, 10 m long and 6 m wide. E, the midpoint of AD, and F, the midpoint of DC, are joined to B. XY is the line joining the midpoints of BF and BC.

(a) Calculate the area of triangle ABE.

Answer ______________________ m^2 (2)

(b) Calculate the area of triangle BFC.

Answer ______________________ m^2 (2)

(c) Hence calculate the area of quadrilateral $BEDF$.

Answer ______________________ m^2 (1)

Multistep questions

Sometimes the structure is not provided by the question and you must decide how to tackle the problem. There are now more of these questions in GCSE papers.

Example 3: Calculate the area of quadrilateral BEDF.

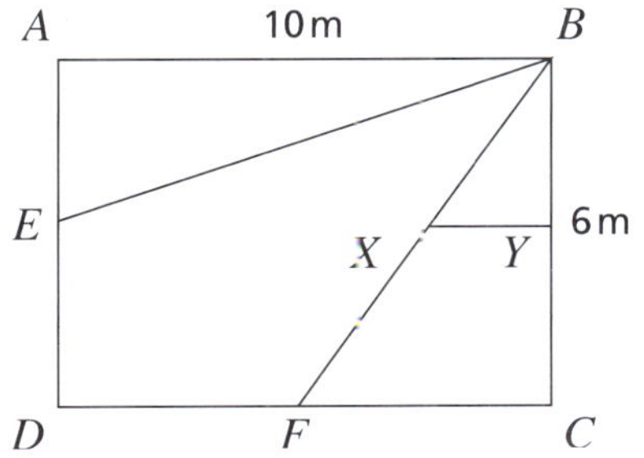

(5)

Non-calculator papers

From 2000, half of GCSE Mathematics papers must be answered without the use of calculating aids. Usually this means that the first paper will be non-calculator. The Mock Paper in this book has been divided into two parts. Questions in this book are shown as:

'Non-calculator' , 'Calculator' or 'possible on either paper' .

Answers to examples:

1: $x = 9$ **2**: (a) $15\,m^2$ (b) $15\,m^2$ (c) $30\,m^2$ **3**: $30\,m^2$

1 Number

REVISION SUMMARY

Questions asked in Number, and the knowledge and skills required to answer them, fall into two broad categories.

The first is **calculation**, firstly without a calculator:

Example 1: Find the cost of 35 books at £3.49 each.

Example 2: $\frac{4}{5} \times \frac{3}{4}$

Example 3: If $\frac{1}{f} = \frac{1}{u} + \frac{1}{v}$ find f when $u = 2$ and $v = 3$.

Example 4: If $x = 4 \times 10^{-3}$ and $y = 5 \times 10^{4}$ find, in standard form, (a) $x \times y$, and (b) $x \div y$.

Or with a calculator:

Example 5: A clock ticks every half second. How many times will it tick in a year?

Substitution into a formula may be required:

Example 6: Find the value of s when

$$s = ut + \frac{1}{2}at^2,\ u = 7.83,\ t = 6,\ a = -0.64$$

The next group of questions are concerned with **estimation**, **approximation** and **errors**.

Questions involving **estimation** may ask for answers to be checked and/or justified.

Example 7: Show that the value of $\frac{17.8 \times 0.53}{0.238}$ is roughly 40.

Estimation is a useful way to check all work on the calculator.

Questions involving **approximation** could include those which ask for answers to be rounded to appropriate degrees of accuracy as well as those involving calculations using approximate numbers. **Errors** arise in questions where, for example, measurements to a given degree of accuracy are involved.

Example 8: 27.3 is correct to 3 significant figures. Write the upper and lower bounds.

Example 9: Cards are made with width 160 mm, to the nearest 5 mm. Envelopes are made with width 162 mm, to nearest millimetre. Will a card always fit in an envelope? Explain your answer.

If you need to revise this subject more thoroughly, see the relevant topics in the *Letts GCSE Mathematics Study Guide* or *CD-ROM*.

Answers to examples:

1: £122.15 2: $\frac{3}{5}$ 3: (a) $1\frac{1}{5}$ or 1.2 4: (a) 2×10^2 (b) 8×10^{-8}

5: 63 072 000 or 6.3072×10^7 6: 35.46 8: 27.25 and 27.35

9: Smallest envelope measures 161.5; largest card measures 162.5. It will not always fit.

Letts Q&A

QUESTIONS

1 Mrs Jones bought 40 scientific calculators costing £7.30 each and some graphical calculators costing £36.80 each. Altogether she spent £660. How many graphical calculators did she buy?

....

Answer ______________________ (2)

2 During the first 3 weeks of life a baby increases its weight from 3.6 kg to 4.5kg. What is the percentage increase?

....

Answer ______________________% (2)

3 Share £140 in the ratio 5 : 2.

....

....

.... (2)

WJEC 1998

4 A car manufacturer reduces the prices of its hatchback from £12 500 to £12 000. What is the percentage reduction?

....

Answer ______________________% (2)

5 If $V = IR$, what is the percentage increase in V when I increases by 10% and R increases by 20%?

....

Answer ______________________% (4)

6 If $P = \sqrt{\frac{V}{Q}}$, find P when $V = 4.6 \times 10^6$ and $Q = 2.8 \times 10^2$. Give your answer in standard form.

....

Answer $P =$ ______________________ (2)

Letts Q&A

QUESTIONS

7 The land area of the Earth's surface is about 4×10^{11} km^2. The population of the Earth is approximately 5000 million.

(a) Write the population of the Earth in standard form.

Answer ______________________ (1)

(b) Calculate the approximate average area, in km^2 per head of population. Give your answer in standard form.

....

Answer ____________________ km^2 (2)

8 Calculate:

(a) $\dfrac{26.78 \times 0.0831}{15.3 \times 6.81}$

(i) Show all the digits on your calculator display.

Answer ______________________ (2)

(ii) Round your answer to a sensible degree of accuracy.

Answer ______________________ (1)

(b) $\dfrac{15.32 + 9.07}{15.32 - 9.07}$

Show all the digits.

Answer ______________________ (2)

9 (a) Arrange these numbers in order, smallest first.

$\frac{1}{3}$, 0.3, 33%, $\frac{3}{11}$.

(2)

(b) Work out

(i) $\frac{4}{5} - \frac{2}{3}$

(ii) $\frac{3}{7} \div \frac{1}{2}$.

(3)

(c) 3827 ÷ 43

(2)

10 I have a small packet to post. To find out how much it will cost, I weigh it.

(a) First I weigh it on scales that weigh to the nearest 10 g.
The packet weighs 70 g.

Write down the smallest that the weight of the packet could be.

Answer ______________________ g (1)

(b) Now I weigh it on electronic scales where the display goes up in 5 g intervals.
The packet weighs 65 g.

Write down the upper and lower bounds of the weight of the package according to the electronic scales.

Upper bound .... g   Lower bound .... g (2)

(c) Finally, I weigh it on a balance to the nearest gram.
It weighs 62 g.

Can all the scales be right? Explain.

.... (2)

11 The formula

$$s = \frac{v^2 - u^2}{2a}$$

gives the distance travelled in metres when the velocity changes from u m/s to v m/s due to a constant acceleration of a m/s^2.

Find s when
$v = 25.0$
$u = 50.0$
$a = -9.8$

....

Answer $s =$ ______________________ m (3)

12 (a) A town has a population of 645 166 people.
The ratio of retired people to the rest of the population is 1 : 3.
How many people are retired?
Give your answer correct to three significant figures.

.... (3)

QUESTIONS

(b) In Britain there are 5.80×10^7 people.
The number of retired people is 1.04×10^7.
What percentage of people in Britain are retired?
Give your answer to an appropriate degree of accuracy.

Answer ______________________ % (3)

SEG 1998

13 Mr Clark borrowed £650 on 1 January 1990. He repaid £243 on 31 December 1990 and the same amount each succeeding 31 December. Compound interest was charged at 6% per annum on the balance during the year. How much was left to pay after 31 December 1992?

....

Answer £ ______________________ (3)

14 At a medical before entering the Army, applicants had their weights and heights recorded.
Peter made a note of his weight and height.
Peter is asked by Farah to tell her his weight and height.
In each part, write down which would be his reply using the most appropriate degree of accuracy.

(a) Peter says his weight is

(i) 83 994 grams (ii) 83.994 kilograms
(iii) approximately 100 kilograms (iv) 84 kilograms

.... (1)

(b) Peter says his height is

(i) approximately 2 metres (ii) 170 centimetres
(iii) 1 metre 70.3 centimetres (iv) 1703 millimetres

.... (1)

MEG 1997

15 When a ball is dropped onto the floor, it bounces and then rises.
This is shown in the diagram.

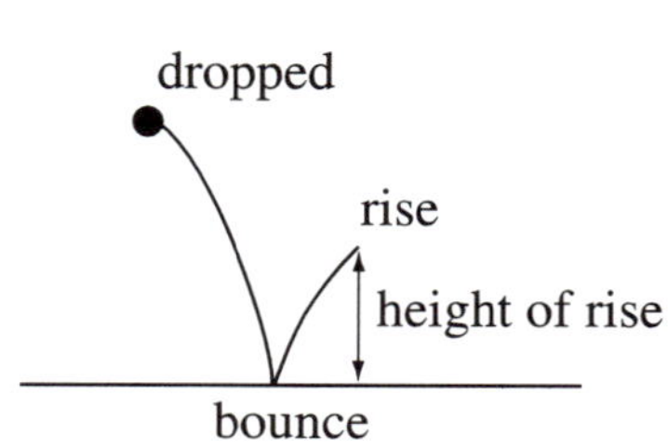

The ball rises to 80% of the height from which it was dropped.
It was dropped from a height of 3 metres.

(a) Calculate the height of the rise after the first bounce.

....

.... (1)

The ball bounces a second time
It rises to 80% of the height of the first rise.

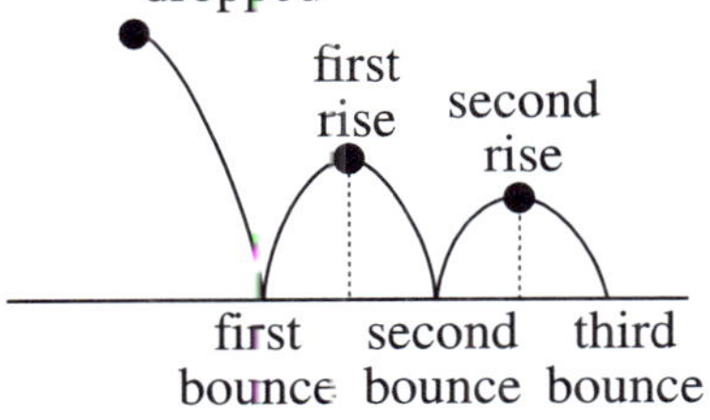

(b) Calculate the height of the second rise.

....

.... (1)

(c) The ball carries on bouncing in this way.
Each time it rises to 80% of the last rise.
For how many bounces does it rise to a height greater than 1 metre?

....

.... (2)

NEAB 1998

16 Sheena weighs 8 stones 6 pounds.

There are 14 pounds in a stone and 1 kilogram is equal to 0.157 stones.

Change Sheena's weight into kilograms.

Give your answer to an appropriate degree of accuracy.

....

....

....

Answer ______________________ kg (4)

SEG 1995

QUESTIONS

17 Supermarkets used to price food in pounds (£) per pound (lb). Here is a label from some cheese.

CHEESE	
£1.72 per lb	
Pack wt	Pack price
10 $\frac{1}{2}$ oz	£1.13

Supermarkets now price food in pounds (£) per kilogram (kg).

Use the conversions 1 kg = 2.2 lb and 1 pound(lb) = 16 ounces (oz) to complete this label for the same pack.

CHEESE	
£.................. per kg	
Pack wt	Pack price
.... g	£1.13

(4)

MEG 1997

REVISION SUMMARY

Questions asked in algebra, and the knowledge and skills required to answer them, fall into three broad categories.

The first is **number patterns and sequences**. It will be necessary to find rules which enable you to continue a number pattern such as 1, 3, 6, 10, 15, … in words or symbols.

Example 1: Find the nth terms of these sequences.
(a) 2, 4, 6, 8, 10, …
(b) 1, 3, 5, 7, 9, …
(c) 2, 8, 18, 32, 50, …

The next group of questions is the largest and involves **solving equations and algebraic manipulation**. Increasing emphasis is being put on this aspect of algebra. At the simplest level it will be necessary to solve equations such as:

Example 2: (a) $5x - 3 = 3 - x$ or (b) $x^2 = 25$

More complex equations will also be set. An equation such as:

Example 3: $x^3 + 2x = 7$

can also be solved by trial and improvement. Graphical methods may also be used, possibly associated with other mathematics. Equations like:

Example 4: $2x - y = 9$
$x + 3y = 8$

may be solved by graphical or algebraic methods. In addition to equations, inequalities must also be solved. These can range from listing whole numbers which satisfy, for example:

Example 5: $-2 < n \leqslant 6$

to finding values of x and y which satisfy

Example 6: $x > 7, y \geqslant 4, x + y \leqslant 20$

Again, solution by graphical or algebraic methods may be required. Such solutions will involve algebraic manipulation but the factorising of expressions such as:

Example 7: (a) $ax^2 + 2bx$ or (b) $x^2 - 3x - 10$

will occur either as part of a longer question or on their own. Expanding (multiplying out brackets) is another skill that could be required and 'changing the subject' of a formula is a regular requirement.

Example 8: make a the subject of $v = u + at$

The last group is concerned with **graphical representation**. The use of coordinates is expected at all levels and this may involve graphical solutions as already mentioned. The interpretation of graphs of simple functions and also of those which represent physical situations, such as speed/time, will be asked.

If you need to revise this subject more thoroughly, see the relevant topics in the *Letts GCSE Mathematics Study Guide* or *CD-ROM*.

Answers to examples:

1: (a) $2n$ (b) $2n - 1$ (c) $2n^2$

2: (a) $x = 1$ (b) $x = 5$ or -5

3: $x = 1.57$

4: $x = 5, y = 1$

5: $-1, 0, 1, 2, 3, 4, 5, 6$

6: many answers possible, for example if $x = 8$ then y would lie between 4 and 12.

7: (a) $x(ax + 2b)$ (b) $(x - 5)(x + 2)$

8: $a = \dfrac{v - u}{t}$

Letts Q&A

QUESTIONS

1 The first 3 terms of a sequence are:
$(3 \times 4) + 1$, $(4 \times 5) + 2$, $(5 \times 6) + 3$.

(a) Write down the next term.

.... (1)

(b) Write down the 6th term.

.... (1)

(c) Write down the nth term, and simplify your answer.

.... (3)

2 Look at this sequence

3, 6, 11, 18, 27, ...

(a) (i) Write down the next two terms in the sequence.

....

Answer ____________ (1)

(ii) Explain how you would find the next term.

.... (1)

(b) Find an expression for the nth term of

(i) 1, 4, 9, 16, 25, ...

....

Answer ____________ (1)

(ii) 3, 6, 11, 18, 27, ...

....

Answer ____________ (2)

3 Look at the three sequences below.

Sequence p 4, 6, 8, 10, 12, ...

Sequence q 3, 8, 15, 24, 35, ...

Sequence r 5, 10, 17, ...

(a) The sequence r is obtained from sequences p and q as follows.

$\sqrt{4^2+3^2}=5$ $\sqrt{6^2+8^2}=10$ $\sqrt{8^2+15^2}=17$ and so on.

(i) Use the numbers 10 and 24 to calculate the fourth term of sequence r.

....

.... (2)

(ii) Calculate the fifth term of sequence r.

....

.... (2)

(b) (i) Find the tenth term of sequence p.

.... (1)

(ii) Find the sixth term of sequence q.

.... (1)

(c) (i) Write down the nth term of sequence p.

....

.... (2)

(ii) The nth term of sequence q is

$$n^2 + kn$$

where k represents a number.

Find the value of k.

.... (1)

NEAB 1995

4 (a) Multiply out the brackets and simplify the expression $(2x + 7)(3x - 6)$.

....

Answer ______________________ (2)

(b) (i) Factorise $x^2 + x - 6$.

....

(ii) Solve the equation $x^2 + x - 6 = 0$.

....

Answer $x =$ ____________________ (4)

5 Solve the following equation:

$$\frac{2x-3}{6} + \frac{x+2}{3} = \frac{5}{2}$$

....

....

....

.... (4)

WJEC 1998

6 John and Sayed are playing a number game:

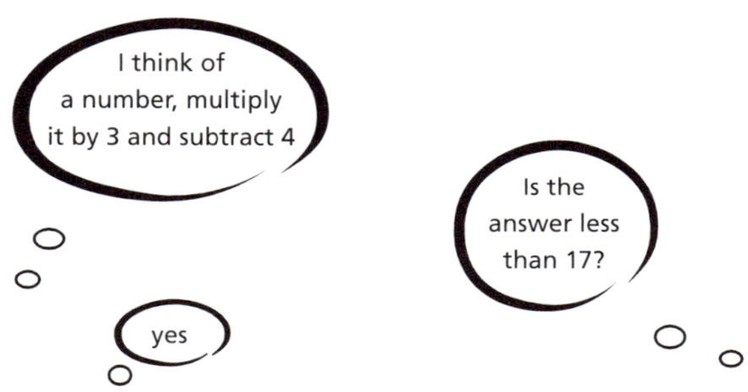

Let n be the number John thought of.

(a) Write down the inequality using n.

Answer ____________________ (1)

(b) Solve the inequality.

....

Answer ____________________ (2)

QUESTIONS

7 The graph of $3y = 2x + 3$ has been drawn on the grid.

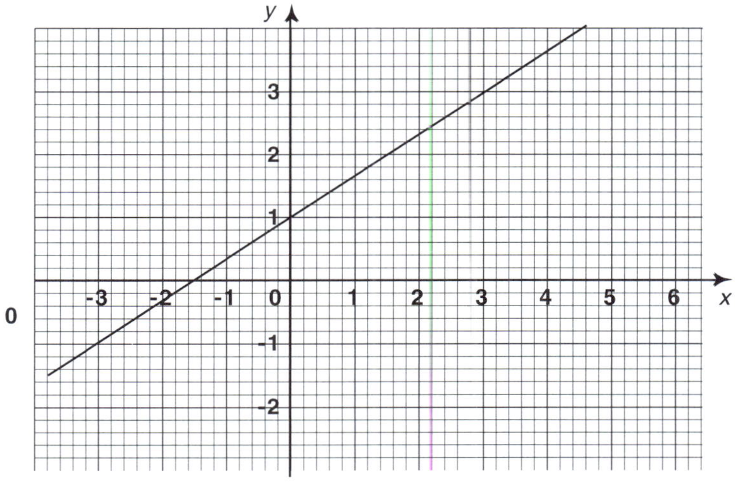

(a) On the same grid draw the graphs of (i) $y = 2x - 2$, (ii) $y = 3 - x$

....

.... (3)

(b) Use the graphs to solve the simultaneous equations $3y = 2x + 3$
$y = 3 - x$

Answer $x =$ ____________________

Answer $y =$ ____________________ (1)

MEG 1996

8 Solve the simultaneous equations:

$$2x + 3y = 17$$
$$3x - 2y = 6.$$

....

....

Answer $x =$ ____________ $y =$ ____________(4)

9 The sum of the squares of the integers from 1 to n is given by

$$s = \frac{1}{6}n(n + 1)(2n + 1).$$

Find s when $n = 10$.

....

Answer $s =$ ____________________ (2)

Letts Q&A

QUESTIONS

10

The traffic capacity of a road can be found by using the following formula:

$$Q = \frac{3600VN}{C}$$

Q = number of vehicles per hour
V = average speed in m/s
N = number of lanes
C = optimum distance between vehicles

(a) Find the capacity of a 2 lane road where the average speed is 12 m/s and the optimum distance is 55 m.

....

Answer Q = ________________ (2)

(b) How many lanes will be needed through a tunnel which will have to take 1000 vehicles an hour, travelling at 15m/s with a spacing of 120 m?

....

Answer N = ________________ (3)

11 To change from Fahrenheit to Celsius we use the formula:

$$C = \tfrac{5}{9}(F - 32)$$

John claims that, on a hot day, the Fahrenheit reading can be exactly double the Celsius reading. At what temperature, Celsius, would this be true?

....

....

Answer ________________ °C (4)

12 The mean and the median of the following numbers are equal. Find x.

30, 40, x, 50, 80.

....

....

Answer x = ________________ (5)

QUESTIONS

13 The *Better Diary Service* supply two kinds of desk diary, the *Page per Day* (PPD) and the *Page per Week* (PPW).
These are two of the orders:

3 PPD	7 PPW	Total cost £53.40
1 PPD	10 PPW	Total cost £50.00

Let d be the price of one PPD in £
w be the price of one PPW in £.

(a) Write down two equations in d and w.

.... (2)

(b) Solve the equations to find the cost of each diary.

....

Answer PPD .... PPW .... (4)

14 Write down all the whole numbers (integers), n, which satisfy

$$-1 < n \leqslant 3.$$

.... (2)

15 Solve the equations
(a) $3x + 2 = 16$,

....

.... (2)

(b) $5(2x - 1) = 35$,

....

.... (2)

(c) $4x + 3 = 18 - 2x$.

....

.... (2)

NEAB 1996

QUESTIONS

16

An old formula gives the distance D miles that can be seen to the horizon when the observer is at height h feet above the sea. The radius of the Earth is r miles and is equal to 3950.

$$D = \sqrt{\frac{2rh}{5280}}$$

Find h when $D = 20$.

....

....

Answer $h =$ ______________ feet (3)

17 Boyle's Law can be stated by the formula

$$P = \frac{k}{V}$$

where P is the pressure and V the volume of a gas.
Transform the formula to make V the subject.

.... (2)

18 Solve the inequalities

(a) $2x - 7 \leqslant 8$.

....

Answer ____________________ (1)

(b) $3 - x > 2$.

....

Answer ____________________ (1)

(c) $x^2 - 4 < 0$.

....

Answer ____________________ (2)

QUESTIONS

19 The equation $x^3 - 5x = 9$ has a solution between 2 and 3.
Use trial and improvement to find this solution correct to two decimal places.
Show all of your trials.

....

....

....

....

.... (4)

MEG 1998

20 I want to make a regular octagon. Each side will be 14 cm. I shall make it from a square piece of card, by cutting off the four corners.

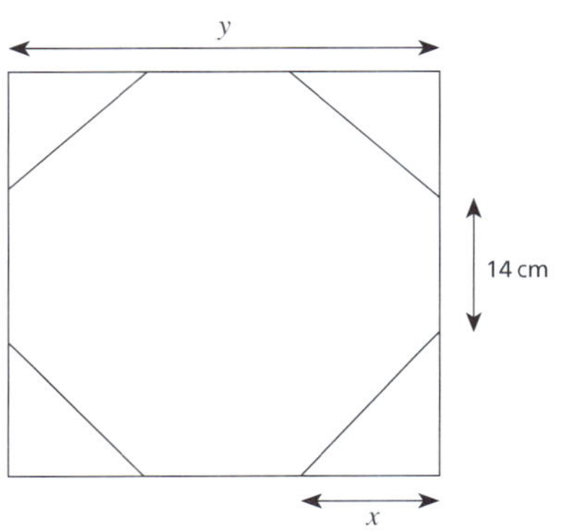

(a) Write down an expression for the area of the octagon in terms of x and y.

....

Answer Area = ______________ (2)

(b) Use Pythagoras to find the value of x.

....

....

Answer x = ______________ (3)

(c) Find the area of the octagon.

....

....

Answer Area = ______________ cm^2 (2)

QUESTIONS

21 (a)

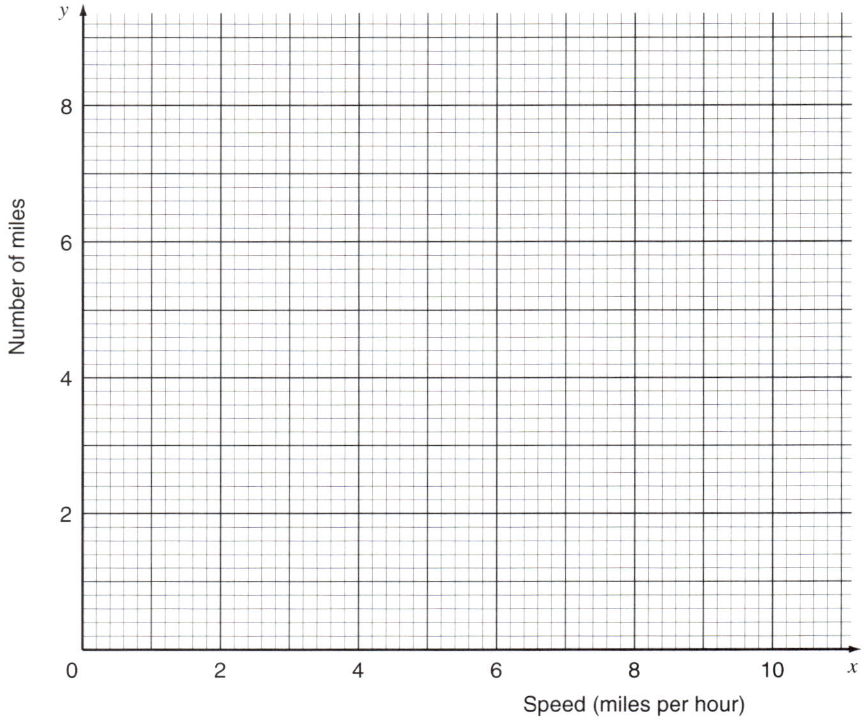

(i) On the grid above draw the lines
$x = 2, \quad y = 4, \quad y = 8 - x.$ (3)

(ii) Shade and label, with the letter R. the region for which the points (x, y) satisfy the three inequalities
$x \geqslant 2, \quad y \leqslant 4, \quad y \leqslant 8 - x.$ (3)

(b) (i) Solve the equation
$5 - 2x = 11.$

Answer .... (2)

(ii) Hence, or otherwise, solve the inequality
$5 - 2x \leqslant 11.$

Answer .... (1)

MEG 1997

QUESTIONS

22 This graph shows the speed of a cyclist as she rides along a hilly road.

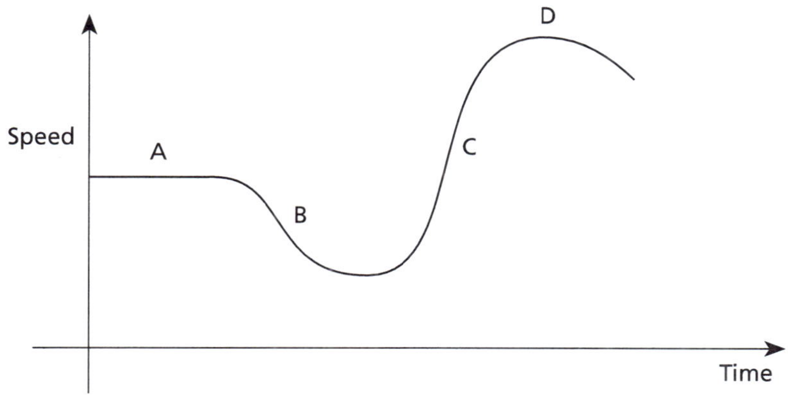

Describe what is happening at A, B, C, D.

A: ....

B: ....

C: ....

D: .... (4)

23 The graph represents a swimming race between Robert and James.

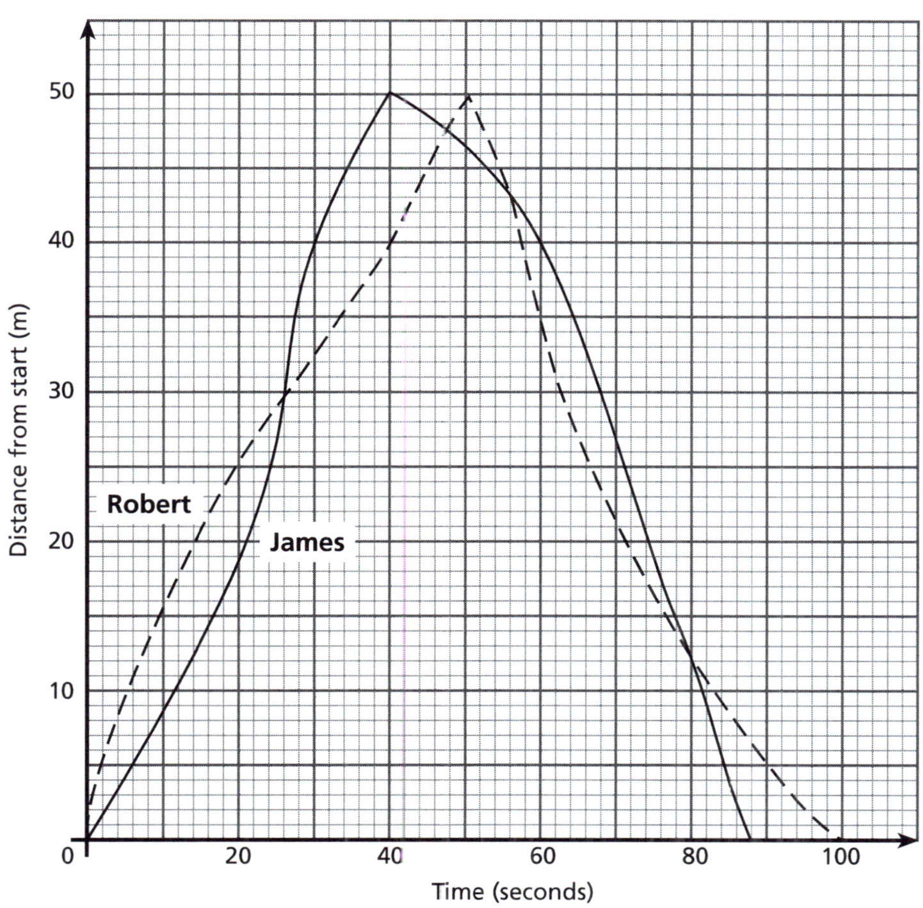

QUESTIONS

(a) At what time did James overtake Robert for the second time?

Answer ________________ seconds (1)

(b) What was the **maximum** distance between the swimmers during the race?

Answer ______________________ m (1)

(c) Who was swimming faster at 56 seconds? How can you tell?

.... (1)

SEG 1995

24 On the axes below draw the graphs of

(a) $y = 4 - x$

(b) $y = x^2$

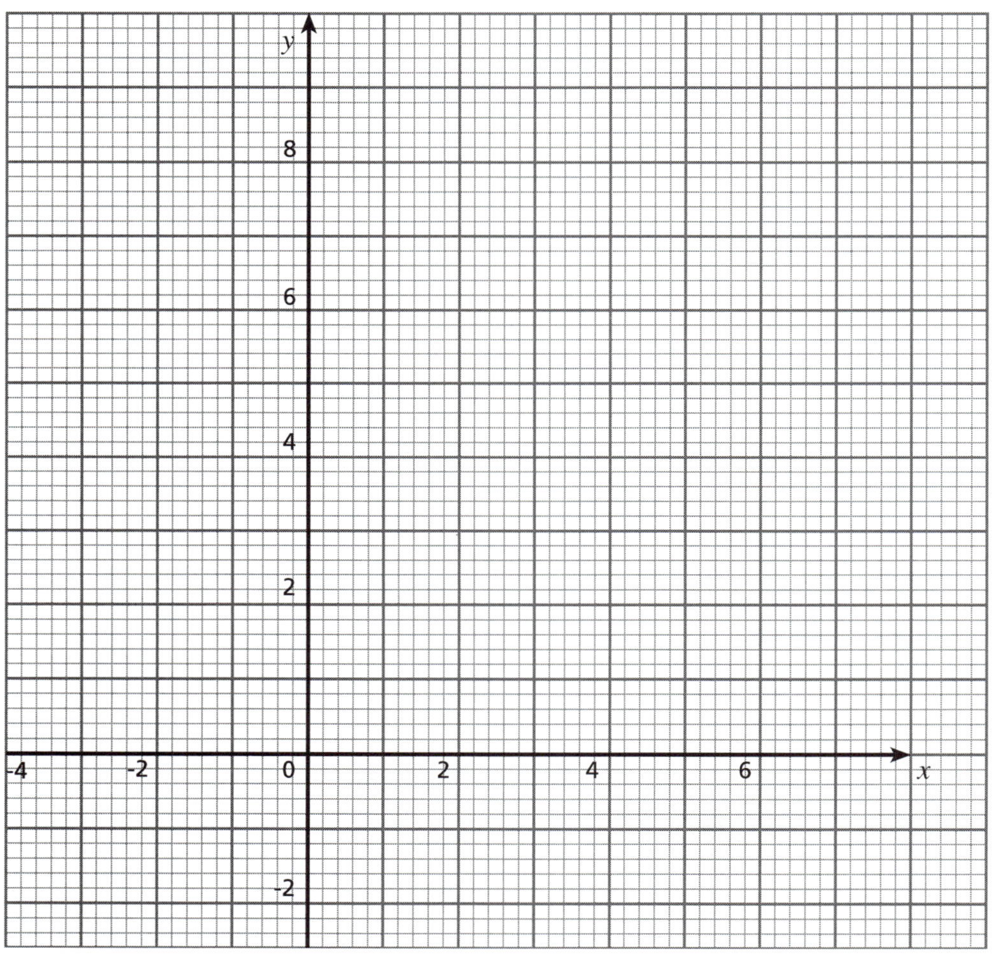

(3)

(c) (i) Write down the values of x where the graphs meet.

Answer $x =$ ____________________ (2)

(ii) Use trial and improvement to find these solutions correct to 2 decimal places.

....

....

....

Answer $x =$ ____________________ (4)

25

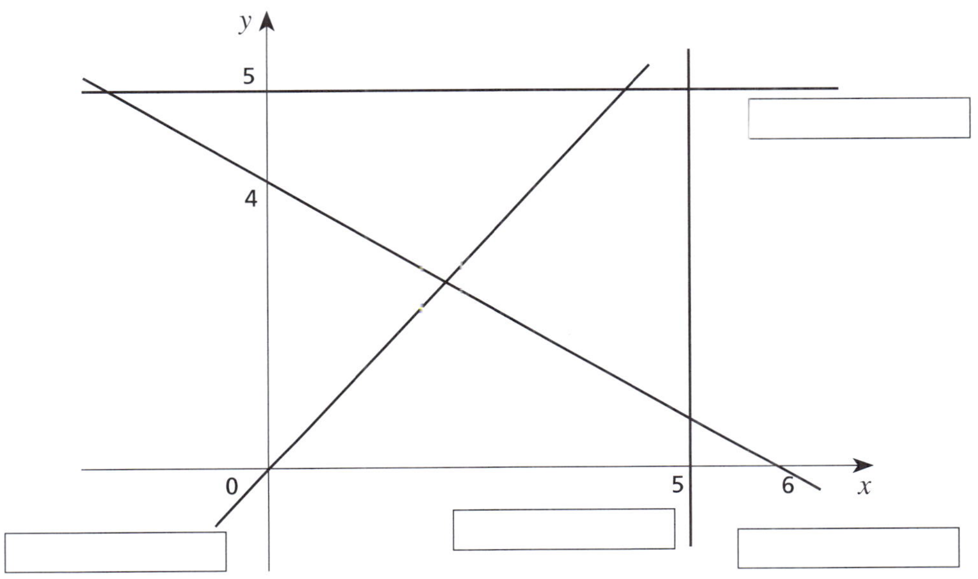

Four lines are drawn on the graph:

$$x = 5, \quad y = 5, \quad 2x + 3y = 12, \quad 2y = 3x.$$

(a) Label the lines by writing the correct equation in each box. (2)

(b) Show, by shading, the region which satisfies

$$x < 5, \quad y < 5, \quad 2x + 3y > 12, \quad 2y < 3x.$$ (2)

QUESTIONS

26 Match each description to a possible sketch graph. In each case label the axes.

A: $y = x^2$ B: $y = x^3$ C: $y = \dfrac{1}{x}$ D: $y + x = 3$

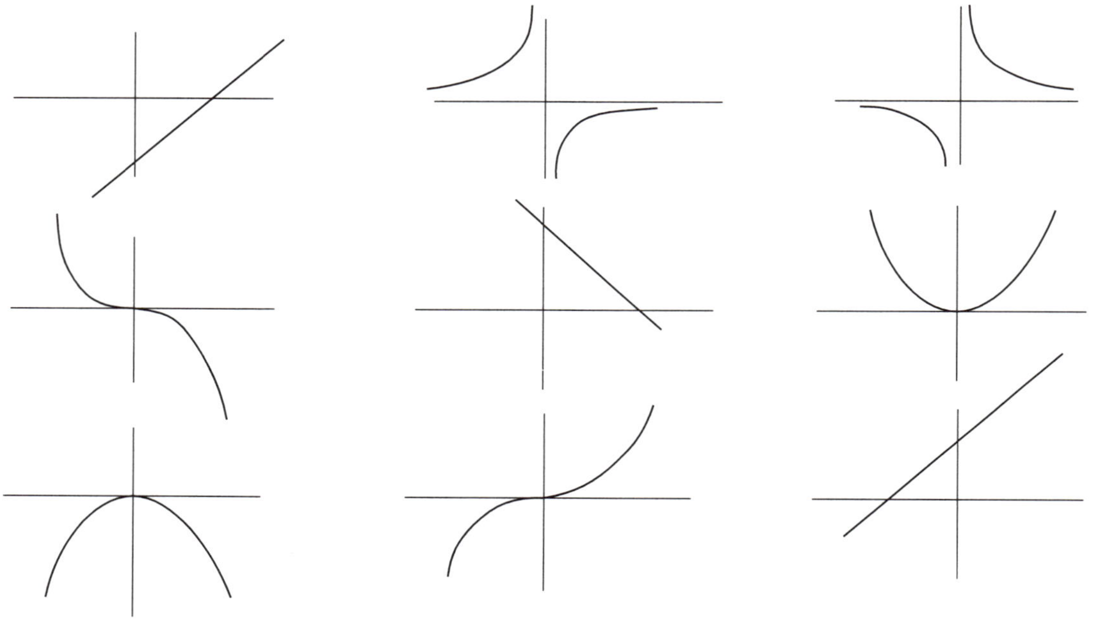

(4)

27

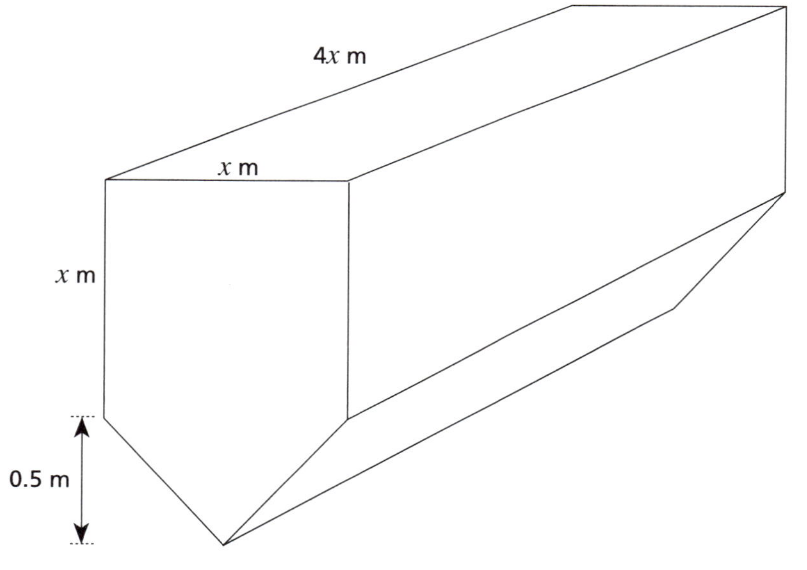

The diagram represents a grain hopper. The hopper is of length $4x$ metres and has a constant cross-section comprised of a square of side x metres and a triangle of perpendicular height 0.5 metres.

(a) Find, in terms of x, the area of the cross-section.

....

....

Answer ______________________ (3)

The hopper can hold 10 m^3 of grain.

(b) Show that $4x^3 + x^2 = 10$.

....

....

.... (3)

(c) Use a trial and improvement method to find the value of x, to one decimal place, for which $4x^3 + x^2 = 10$.

....

....

....

Answer $x =$ ______________________ (4)

NICCEA 1995

28 (a) Expand the following expression, simplifying your answer as far as possible.

$$(3x - 4)(x + 2)$$

....

.... (2)

(b) Factorise the expression:

$$5ab + 10b^2$$

....

.... (2)

(c) Make d the subject of the formula:

$$c = 2\text{a} - 4d$$

....

.... (2)

WJEC 1997

3 Shape, space and measures

REVISION SUMMARY

There are three main groups of questions in this attainment target plus some other types of question at the higher levels.

The first group is those concerned with **Pythagoras's Theorem and trigonometry in 2-D and 3-D shapes**.

Here questions such as:

Example 1: Find the length of the sides AC and AB and the size of the angle BCA in the following triangle.

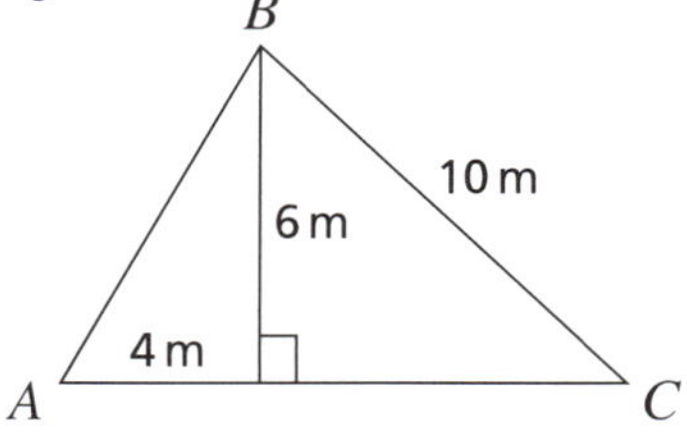

could appear but are often set in a context.

The next group involves the calculation of **areas and volumes of 2-D and 3-D shapes**.

You are expected to know the formulae for the area and circumference of a circle ($A = \pi r^2$, $C = 2\pi r$ or πd) and will be given the formulae for the areas and volumes of shapes such as the trapezium, cone and sphere.

Example 2: A child's clown toy is made from a cone attached to a hemisphere of radius 5 cm. If the total height of the toy is 20 cm find its volume.

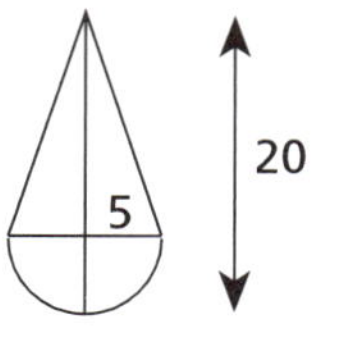

The third group of questions are those concerned with **position** and **locus**. These will include bearings – to define direction – and the use of coordinates in two and three dimensions to locate position.

Example 3: A cuboid has its edges parallel to the axes. Its dimensions are 3, 2, 1 units. One vertex is at (2, 3, 0). Find a possible position for the opposite vertex.

Example 4: Jane rows her boat under a bridge.
She keeps the same distance from two bridge supports, A and B.
Describe the locus of the boat.

The final – mixed – group will include questions concerned with **geometry** for example:

- the conditions for congruent triangles;
- enlarging shapes, similar shapes, surface area and volume of similar shapes.

Answers to examples:

1: $AB = 7.2$ cm; $AC = 12$ cm; angle $BCA = 36.9°$
2: volume = 654 cm^3
3: e.g.: (0, 0, 1), but many others
4: a straight line bisecting AB at right angles

If you need to revise this subject more thoroughly, see the relevant topics in the *Letts GCSE Mathematics Study Guide* or *CD-ROM*.

1 The diagram shows a triangular prism.

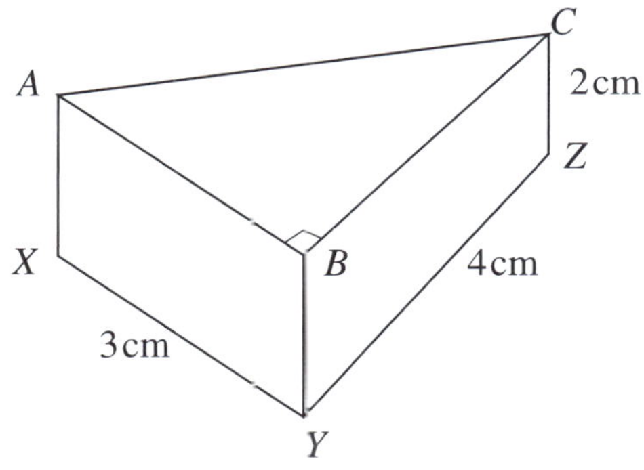

Angle $ABC = 90°$
$XY = 3$cm, $YZ = 4$cm and $CZ = 2$cm.

(a) Calculate the volume of the prism, stating your units.

....

....

....

.... (4)

(b) One face of the prism, $BCZY$, has been drawn below.
Complete an accurate net of the prism. (3)

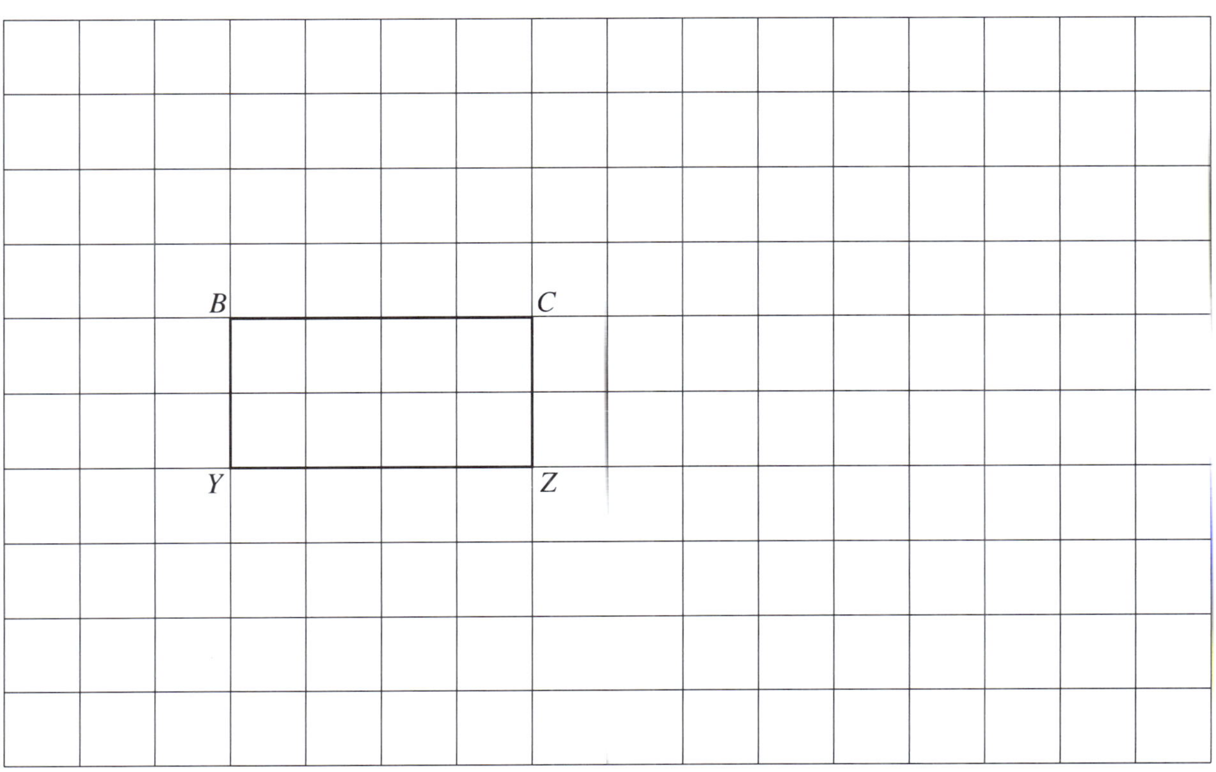

SEG 1998

QUESTIONS

2 The logo for a company consists of 2 small circles inside a larger circle, as shown. The two inside circles have radii of 2 cm and 3 cm.

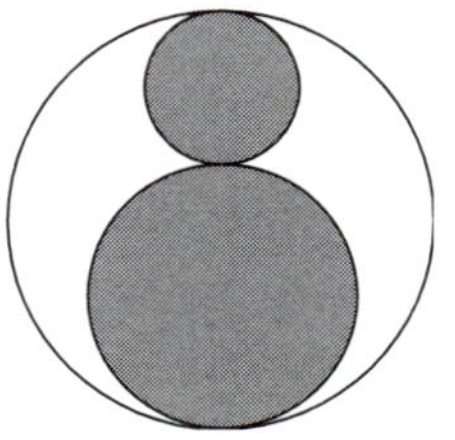

(a) Find the radius of the large circle.

....

Answer ____________________ cm (2)

(b) Find the shaded area.

....

Answer ____________________ cm^2 (3)

3 Two circular discs are cut out of a rectangular sheet of metal. What is the area of metal left?

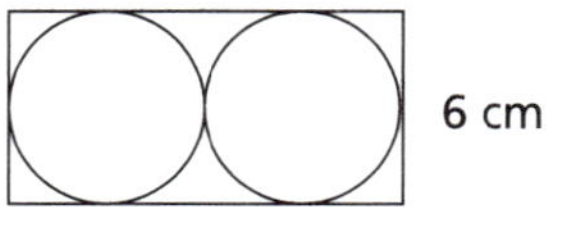

....

Answer ____________________ cm^2 (5)

4 The bottom of this swimming pool slopes evenly from a depth of 2 m at the shallow end to 4 m at the deep end.

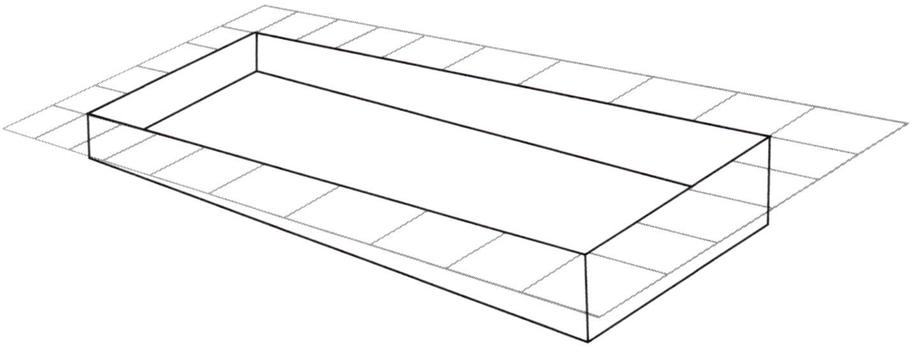

The pool is 25 m long and 15 m wide. Find its volume.

....

....

Answer ____________________ m^3 (4)

QUESTIONS

5 In the diagram AB is parallel to CD.
$AB = OC = 12\text{cm}$. $OB = 10\text{cm}$.

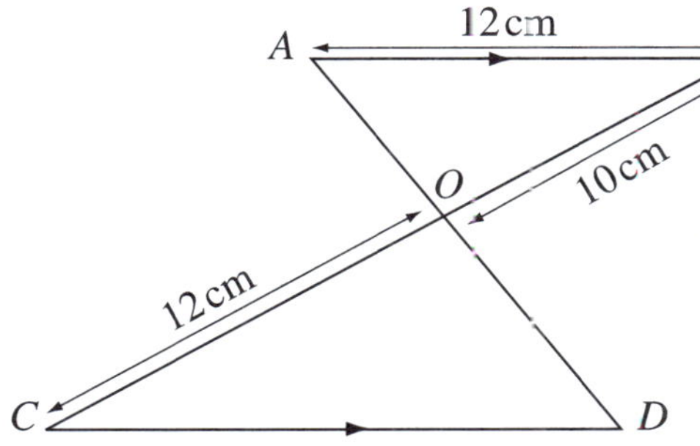

Not drawn to scale

Use similar triangles to calculate the length of CD.

....

....

....

.... (3)

NEAB 1998

6 The diagram shows a running track with the 'straights' 90 m long and with semicircular end sections. If the inside distance is 400 m and the track is 8 m wide, how much further is it to run round the outside of the track?

....

....

Answer ______________________ m (5)

QUESTIONS

7

A new tube of toothpaste is roughly a cylinder, diameter 3.0 cm, length 14.5 cm.

(a) Calculate the volume of toothpaste in the tube.

....

....

Answer ____________ cm^3 (2)

The toothpaste is squeezed through a circular hole, diameter 7 mm. Each time I clean my teeth, I use a 'cylinder' of length 15 mm.

(b) How many times can I clean my teeth from this tube?

....

....

Answer ____________ (4)

8 In a school hall, the stage is lit by a spotlight fixed to a wall.

The spotlight is 4.35 metres up the wall and is set to shine on a spot on the stage 5.2 metres away from the wall, as shown in the diagram.

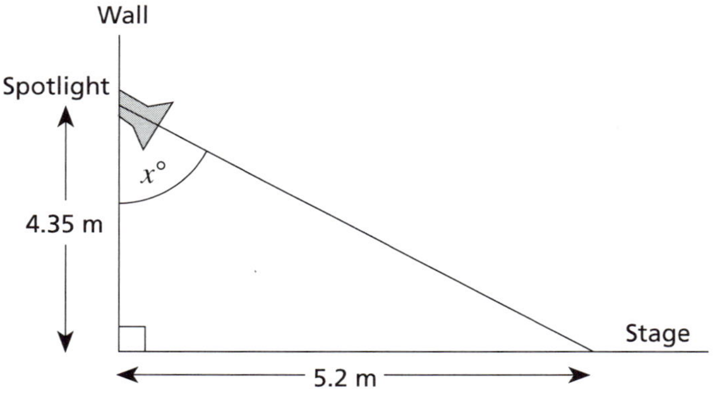

Calculate the size of the angle marked $x°$.

Do not use a scale drawing.

....

....

.... (4)

SQA 1995

QUESTIONS

9 Find the unknown lengths in these right-angled triangles.

(a)

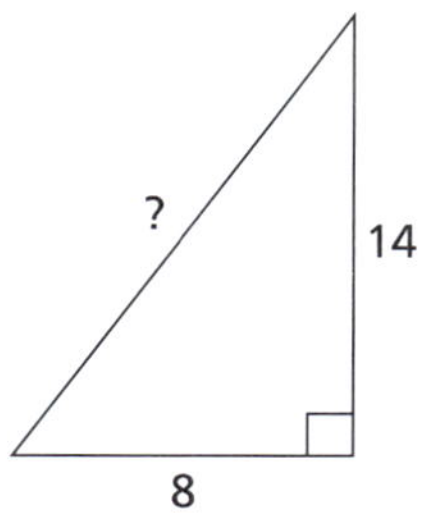

....

....

....

Answer ______________________ (3)

(b)

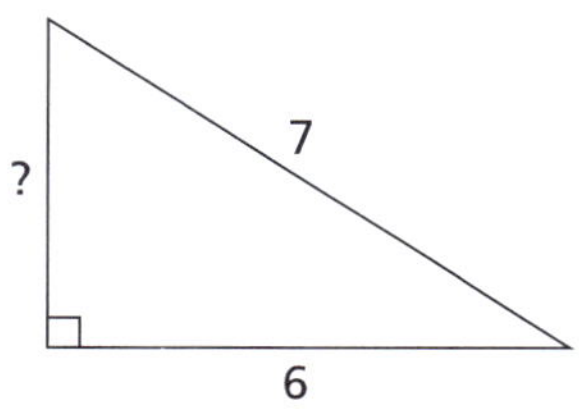

....

....

Answer ______________________ (3)

10

DO NOT USE THIS LADDER AT ANGLES MORE THAN 70° TO THE HORIZONTAL

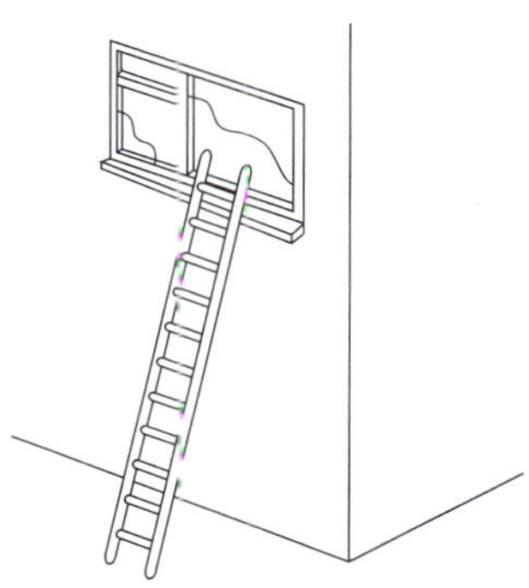

Gurpal's ladder is 5.50 m long.

(a) If it stands on horizontal ground, how far up the wall can it reach?

....

Answer ______________________ m (3)

(b) How far will the foot of the ladder then be from the wall?

....

Answer ______________________ m (3)

Mark also has a ladder. Its length can be extended. He puts his ladder with the foot 1.80 m from the wall. It makes an angle of 67° with the ground.

(c) How far up the wall will it reach?

....

....

Answer ______________________ m (3)

QUESTIONS

11

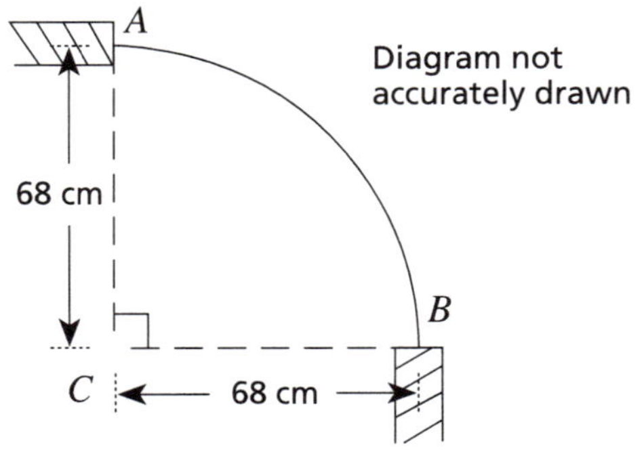

The diagram represents the plan of a window frame.
The arc *AB* is a quarter of a circle.
The centre of the circle is at *C* and the radius of the circle is 68 cm.

(a) Calculate the length of the arc *AB*.

(Use $\pi = 3.14$ or use the π button on your calculator.)
Give your answer correct to 3 significant figures.

....

....

Answer ____________________ cm (3)

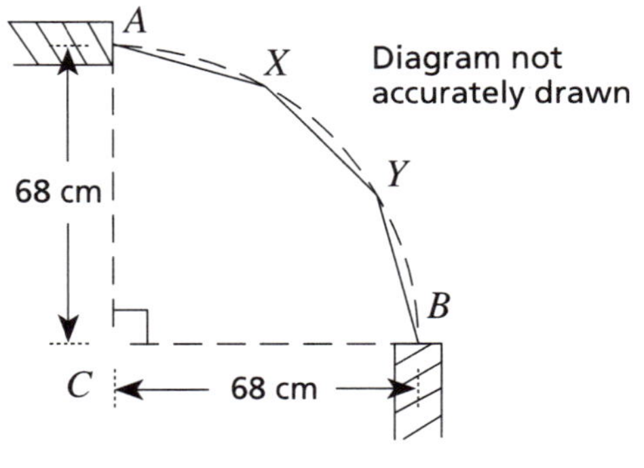

The window frame in part (a) is replaced by double glazed panels.
These panels are made only in straight lengths.
The arc *AB* is replaced by three identical panels *AX*, *XY* and *YB*.

(b) Calculate the length of *AX*.
Give your answer correct to 2 significant figures.

....

....

....

Answer ____________________ cm (4)

Edexcel 1995

12 (a) Find the area of trapezium PQRS.

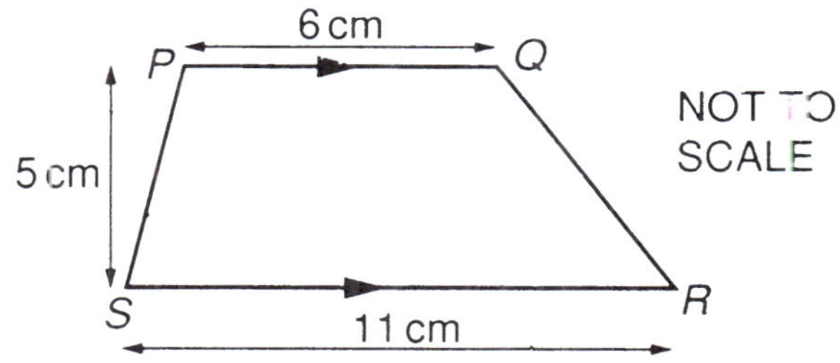

.... (2)

(b) (i) Use your calculator to work out the height, h, of a trapezium when

$$h = \frac{2 \times 50.65}{3.61 + 5.23}.$$

Give your answer correct to two decimal places.

.... (3)

(ii) Show how you would check, **without using your calculator**, that your answer to part **(b)(i)** is reasonable.

.... (3)

(c) *ABCD* is a trapezium.

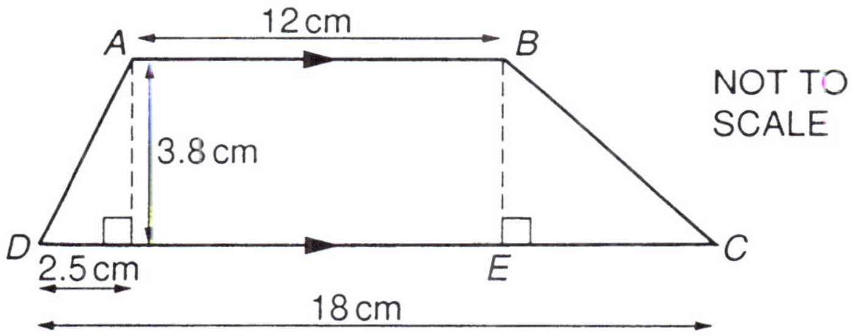

(i) Find the length of *AD*.

.... (3)

E is the foot of the perpendicular from *B* to *DC*.

(ii) Find the length of *EC*.

.... (1)

(iii) Calculate angle *BCE*.

.... (3)

MEG 1997

QUESTIONS

13 Pauline is building a greenhouse.

The base, *PQRS* of the greenhouse should be a rectangle measuring 2.6 m by 1.4 m.

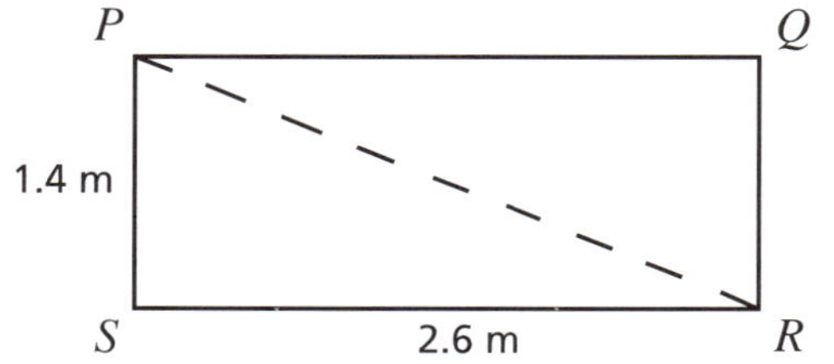

Not to scale

To check the base is rectangular Pauline has to measure the diagonal *PR*.

(a) Calculate the length of *PR* when the base is rectangular.
You **must** show all your working.

....

Answer ______________________ m (3)

(b) When building the greenhouse Pauline finds angle $PSR > 90°$. She measures *PR*.

Which of the following statements is **true**?

X: *PR* is greater than it should be.
Y: *PR* is less than it should be.
Z: *PR* is the right length.

Answer ______________________ (1)

SEG 1995

14

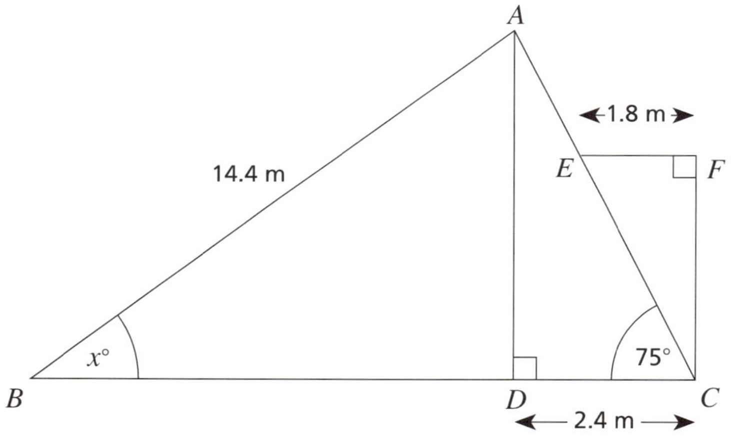

Not to scale

The diagram represents a triangular roof frame *ABC* with a window frame *EFC*.

BDC and *EF* are horizontal and *AD* and *FC* are vertical.

(a) Calculate the height *AD*.

....

Answer $AD =$ ________________ m (3)

(b) Calculate the size of the angle marked $x°$ in the diagram.

....

Answer $x =$ ____________________ (3)

(c) Calculate FC.

....

Answer $FC =$ ________________ m (3)

MEG 1995

15 A party of hikers is walking across open moorland using a compass.

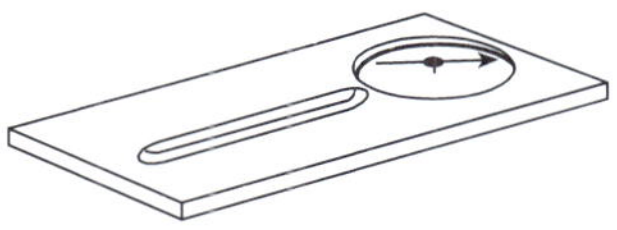

They have been walking on a bearing of 326°. They decide to turn back and retrace their steps.

(a) On what bearing should they walk?

....

Answer ________________________ (1)

Near the end of the walk there is a steep descent. Lesley decides to check the gradient from the map.

The top has height 293 m and $\frac{1}{2}$ km further on they cross the 150 m contour.

(b) What is the average gradient?

....

Answer ________________________ (2)

16 This diagram shows a sail $ABDC$.

AC is 4.5m long.
AB is 4.2m long.
Angle DAC is 26°.
AD is perpendicular to BC.

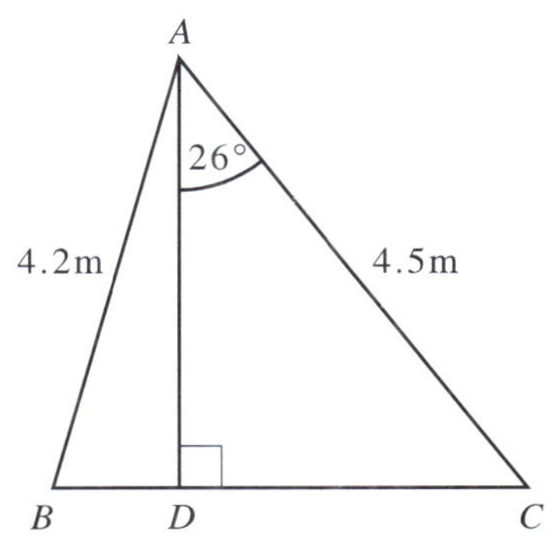

(a) Calculate the height, AD, of the sail.

.... (3)

QUESTIONS

(b) Calculate angle ABD.

.... (2)

WJEC 1996

17 Here are some expressions associated with a sphere:

$$\tfrac{4}{3}\pi r^3,\ \pi h^2\left(r-\frac{h}{3}\right),\ 2\pi rk,\ 2\pi r^2.$$

(r, h, k are all lengths)
Which of these expressions could be areas? Explain.

....

Answer ______________________ (2)

18 (a) Water is being poured at a constant rate into a container which has the shape of a prism.
The diagram shows the cross-section of the container.
Sketch a graph to show the height of water in the container as it is being filled.

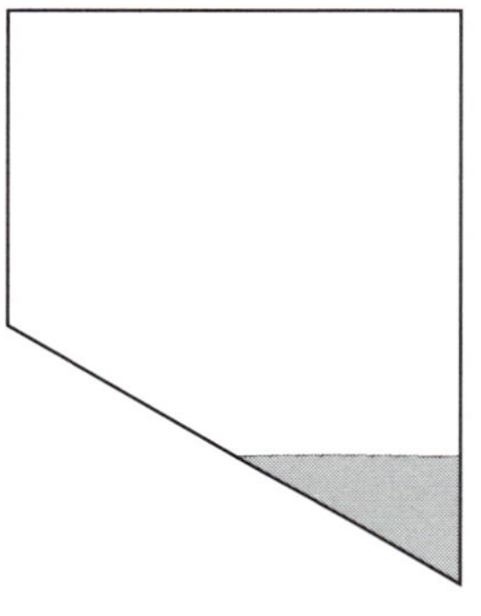

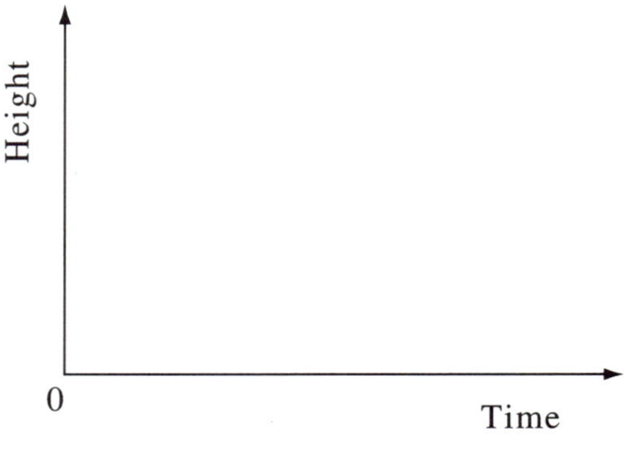

(2)

(b) Another view of the container is shown.

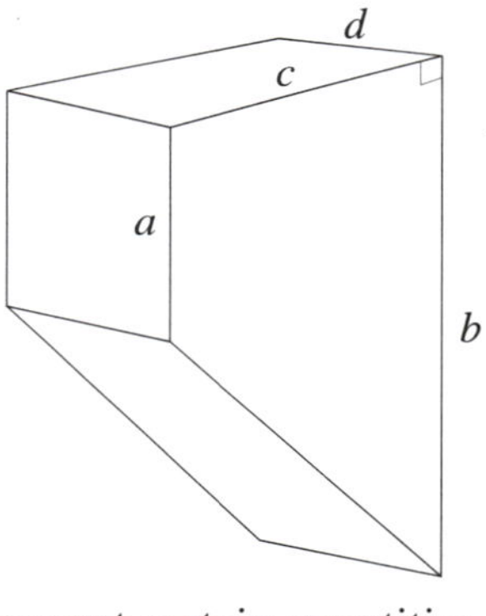

The following formulae represent certain quantities connected with the container.

$$2(a+b) \qquad \tfrac{1}{2}(a+b)c \qquad \tfrac{1}{2}(a+b)cd$$

Which of these formulae represents area?

.... (1)

SEG 1998

QUESTIONS

19 The diagram shows a wooden frame for a doorway. The frame consists of three sides of a rectangle and a semicircle.

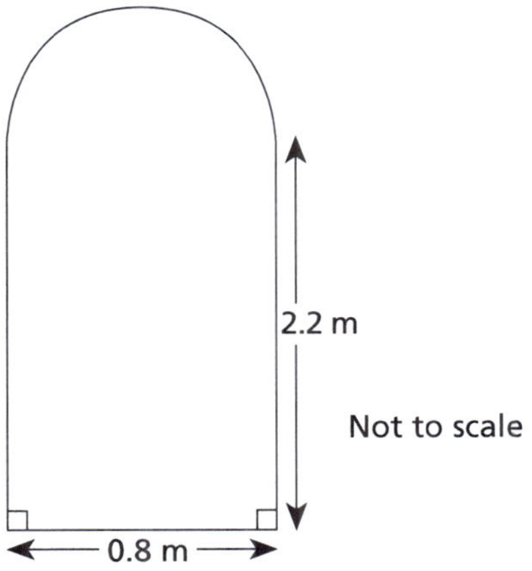

(a) (i) Calculate the length of a semicircle of diameter 0.8 m.

....

Answer ______________________ m (2)

(ii) Calculate the perimeter of the frame.

Answer ______________________ m (1)

(b) While the frame was being fitted into a building it was held in place by supports.

The diagram below shows two of the supports, *AB* and *CD*. *DEA* is horizontal.

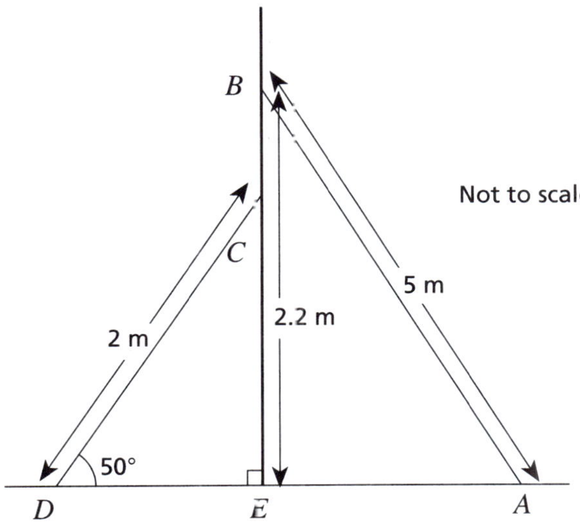

QUESTIONS

(i) Calculate the length of *AE*.

....

Answer ____________________ m (3)

(ii) Calculate the length of *DE*.

....

Answer ____________________ m (2)

MEG 1995

20 The diagram represents the windscreen wiper on a bus.

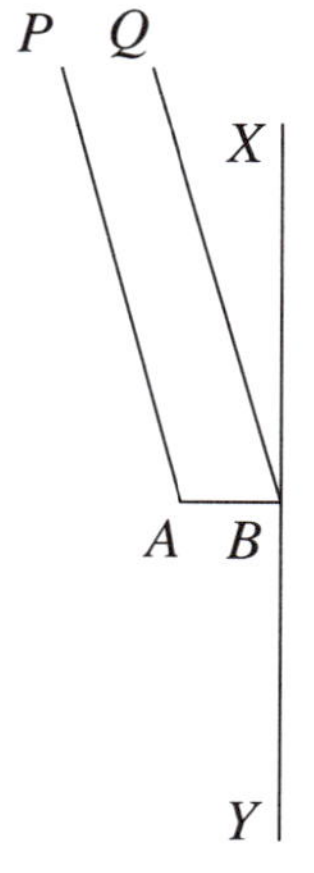

It is made of three rigid arms, *PA*, *QB* and *AB*. They are loosely jointed at *A* and *B*. *XY* is the wiper blade and is rigidly fixed to *AB* at right angles.

PA = *QB* and *AB* = *PQ*. *P* and *Q* are pivots fixed to the bus and *PQ* is horizontal. The arm *QB* rotates about *Q* and the arm *PA* rotates about *P*.

(a) Explain why *AB* stays horizontal as *QB* rotates.

.... (1)

(b) Describe the locus of (i) *B* and (ii) *X*.

B ....

X .... (2)

QB rotates in each direction in turn, stopping when it makes an angle of 40° with the vertical.

(c) Sketch the shape wiped by the blade *XY*.

(2)

QUESTIONS

21 (a) The diagram below is the plan of a campsite drawn to a scale of 1 centimetre to 5 metres.

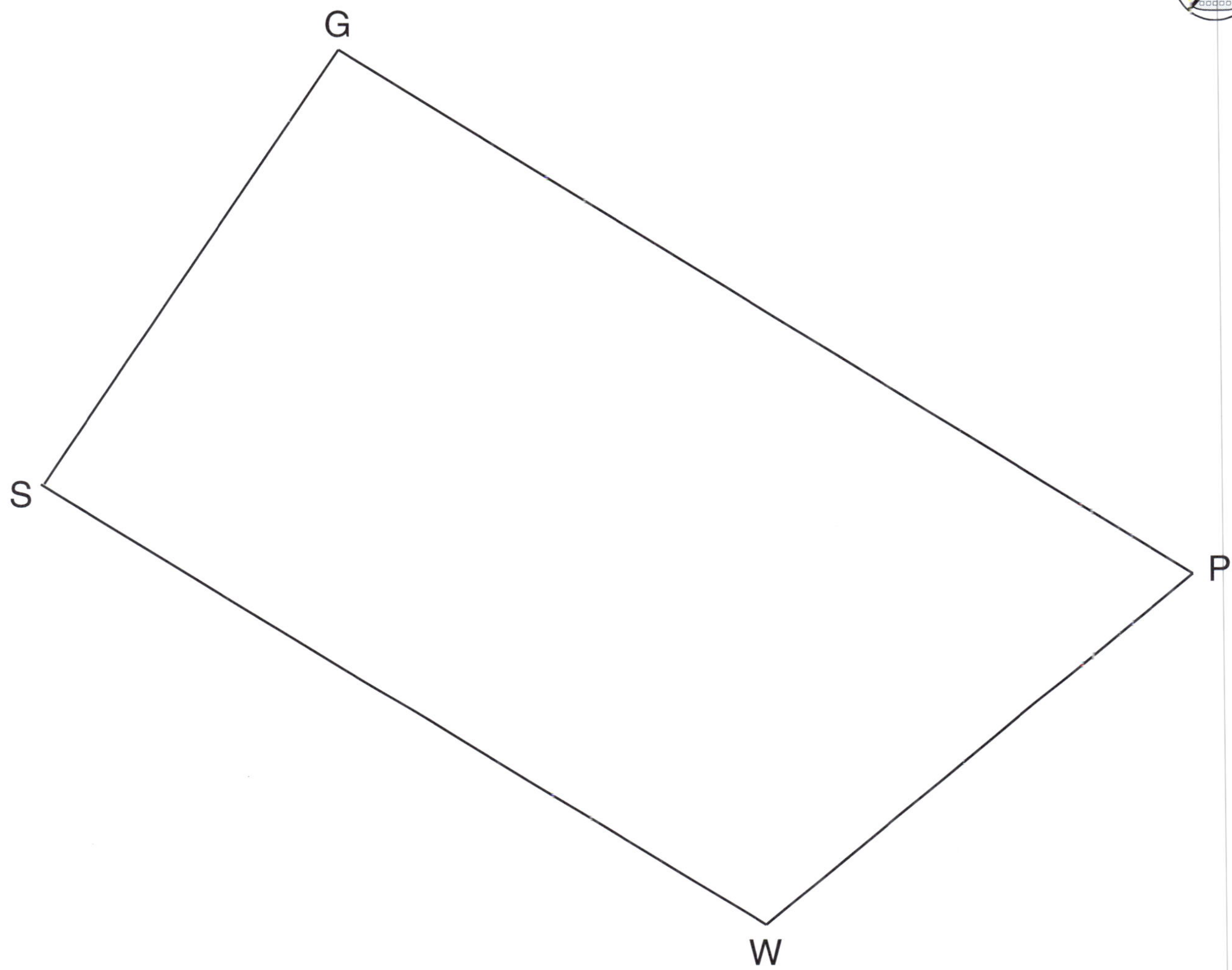

The campsite owner decides to put a new water tap on the campsite.
The tap must be the same distance from the shop, *S*, as it is from the gate, *G*.

(i) Draw accurately the locus of all points equidistant from *G* and *S*. (2)

The water system is such that the tap must be no more than 50 metres from the wash-block, *W*.

(ii) Construct accurately the locus of points which are exactly 50 m from *W*. (2)

(iii) Show on the diagram all possible positions for the tap. (1)

QUESTIONS

(b) The campsite has a children's pool and a main pool.
The main pool is an enlargement of the children's pool.

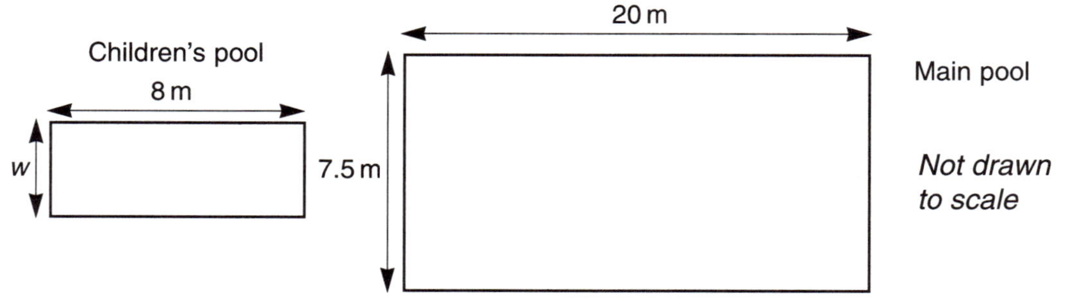

(i) Find the scale factor of the enlargement.

....

....

.... (2)

(ii) Find the width, w, of the children's pool.

....

....

.... (2)

MEG 1997

Handling data

REVISION SUMMARY

There are two main sections in this attainment target – **collecting, processing and interpreting data** and **probability**.

Questions involving the **processing and interpreting of information** may include the drawing of graphs – e.g. frequency diagrams and cumulative frequency curves and using these to estimate median and interquartile range, as well as the drawing of bar charts and pie charts. The median and mode, as well as the mean, may, in some questions, have to be calculated.

Example 1: The table shows the heights of 50 eight-year-old boys. Calculate estimates for (a) the mean height and (b) the median height of the boys.

Height (h cm)	Number
$96 \leqslant h < 100$	1
$100 \leqslant h < 104$	3
$104 \leqslant h < 108$	8
$108 \leqslant h < 112$	12
$112 \leqslant h < 116$	13
$116 \leqslant h < 120$	7
$120 \leqslant h < 124$	4
$124 \leqslant h < 128$	2

Questions concerned with **probability** will extend from straightforward ones such as:

Example 2: Find the probability of drawing a black ball from a bag containing 10 black balls, 15 red balls and 20 green balls.

Example 3: The probability that my train will be late is 0.35. What is the probability that it will not be late?

to more involved ones:

Example 4: A bag contains 8 red marbles and 6 yellow marbles. Three marbles are taken from the bag at random and not replaced. Find the probability of drawing (a) three red ones, (b) three yellow ones and (c) at least one red marble.

If you need to revise this subject more thoroughly, see the relevant topics in the *Letts GCSE Mathematics Study Guide* or *CD-ROM*.

Answers to examples:

1: mean = [98 × 1 + 102 × 3 + …] ÷ 50 = 112.4 cm,
median (between 25th and 26th) is just in the interval $112 \leqslant h < 116$ = 112 cm

2: $\frac{2}{9}$

3: 0.65

4: $\frac{2}{13}$, $\frac{5}{91}$, $\frac{86}{91}$

Letts Q&A

QUESTIONS

1 Alfalfa (or lucerne) is a plant used for animal fodder and the extraction of chlorophyll. It can be grown in water.

An experiment was conducted, growing alfalfa in various depths of water. The table shows the results:

Depth of water (cm)	30	45	60	75	90	105	120
Yield of alfalfa (tonnes/hectare)	13.1	14.1	15.6	17.8	20.3	21.5	20.8

(a) Draw a scatter diagram for these data. (2)

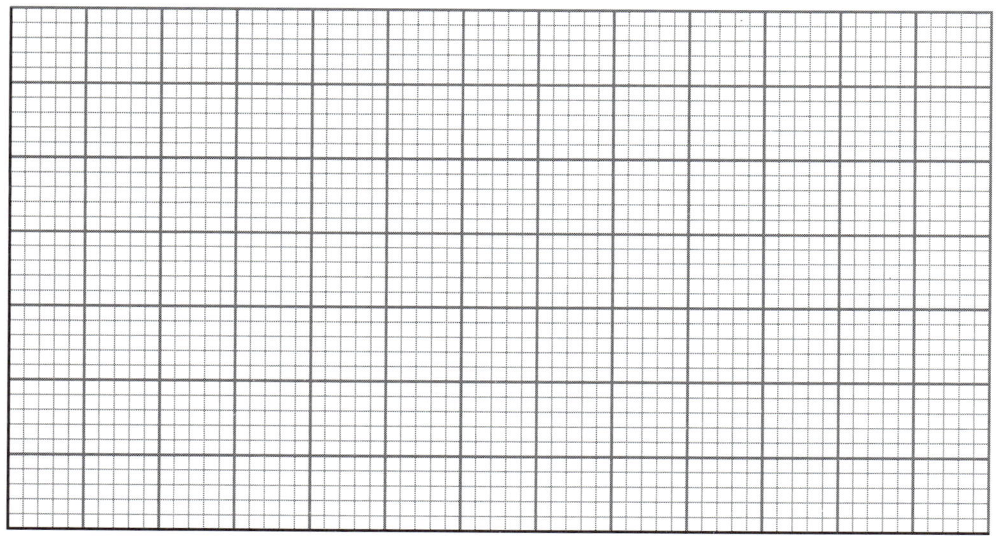

(b) Draw a line of best fit on the diagram. (1)

(c) Estimate the yield for a depth of 100 cm.

Answer ____________ tonnes/hectare (1)

(d) Why would you not use your line to estimate the yield at depth 150 cm?

.... (2)

2 The salaries of 8 employees working in a department of a large company are as follows:

£21 000 £23 500 £27 500 £36 000 £19 000 £23 500 £19 000 £19 000

(a) Find the mean, median and mode of their salaries.

....

Mean = £ __________ Median = £ __________ Mode = £ __________ (3)

(b) Which one does not give a good indication of their average salary? Why?

.... (1)

3 (a) A headline in a newspaper this year stated:

> **Students skip Breakfast!**
>
> *Our survey shows that few students are eating cereals, fruit, or bread for breakfast.*
>
> **In fact they eat nothing at all!**

You are asked to conduct a survey to find out what students eat for breakfast.

Design an observation sheet to collect the data you need.

Invent the first 20 entries on your data sheet (3)

(b) The newspaper made the following statement about the eating habits of teenagers.

> Only one in a hundred teenagers eat fruit and vegetables each day. Over half eat no vegetables other than chips

You are asked to find out whether this statement is true in your area.
Give three questions you could ask teenagers to see if what the article says is true in your area.

....

....

.... (3)

NEAB 1995

4 A historian is comparing the populations of England and Wales in 1881 and 1951.
These are the distributions for the male population (in 1000's):

Age	Mid-value	Number of men 1881	Number of men 1951	Cumulative frequency 1881	Cumulative frequency 1951
Under 15		4740	3785		
15 and under 30		3380	4150		
30 and under 45		2250	4639		
45 and under 60		1430	3722		
60 and under 75		710	2232		
75 and over		110	534		

(Take the mid-value of the '75 and over' group to be 82.5, that is everyone is under 90.)

(a) (i) Draw the two frequency polygons on the same axes. Label each.

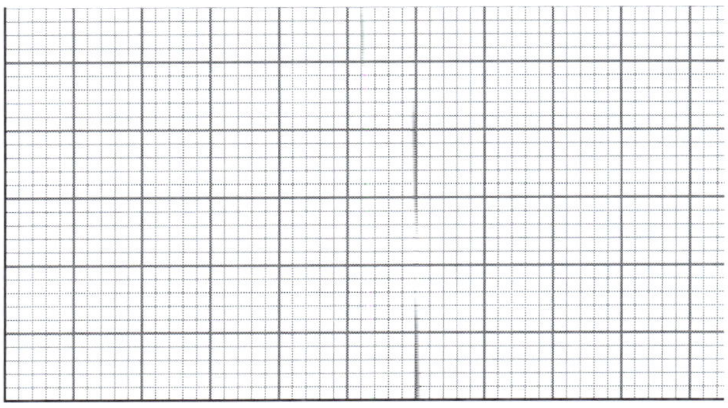

(4)

QUESTIONS

(ii) Calculate the estimates of mean ages in 1881 and 1951.

....

Mean age (1881) ________________ (2)

....

Mean age (1951) ________________ (2)

(iii) Comment on the differences between the two distributions.

.... (2)

(b) (i) Use the spare columns to write down the cumulative frequencies. (2)

(ii) Draw the cumulative frequency curves on the same axes below. Label each. (4)

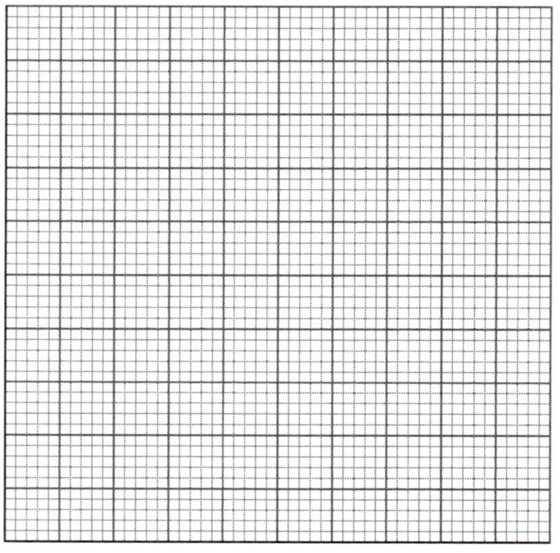

(c) Use the curves to find, for each year,

(i) the median ages,

(ii) the interquartile ranges,

(iii) the percentages of the male populations over 21.

....

Answers:

	Median	**IQ range**	**% over 21**
1881			
1951			

(6)

(d) Comment on any other differences.

.... (2)

5 The table gives the average temperature and rainfall for ten weeks in Bukosa.

Average rainfall (mm)	39	45	29	33	35	19	18	30	9	5
Average temperature (°C)	17	21	27	21	24	32	37	33	36	41

(a) Complete the scatter graph for these data. (2)

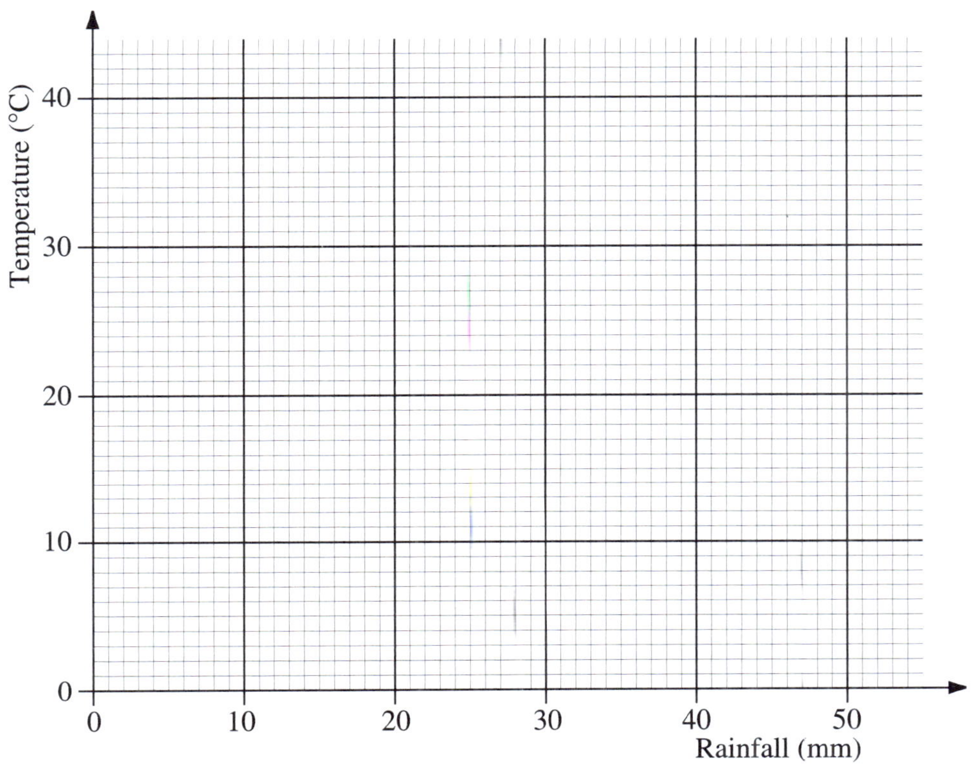

(b) Comment on the correlation.

....

.... (1)

(c) Draw the line of best fit on the graph. (1)

(d) Use the graph to estimate the rainfall during a week when the average temperature is 29°C.

.... mm (1)

MEG 1998

QUESTIONS

6 A survey was made of the time spent by each of 500 customers at the check-outs of a supermarket. The results were recorded in the frequency table.

Time (t minutes)	Frequency
$0 < t \leqslant 1$	83
$1 < t \leqslant 2$	138
$2 < t \leqslant 3$	141
$3 < t \leqslant 4$	68
$4 < t \leqslant 5$	45
$5 < t \leqslant 6$	25

(a) Calculate the mean time spent by each customer at the check-out.

....

Answer ________________ minutes (4)

(b) Complete the cumulative frequency table.

Time (less than or equal to) minutes	Cumulative frequency
1	83
2	
3	
4	
5	
6	

(3)

(c) Draw the cumulative frequency curve on the graph paper on the next page. (4)

(d) Use the graph to estimate

(i) the median time,

Answer ________________ minutes (1)

(ii) the interquartile range.

Answer ________________ minutes (2)

Letts Q&A

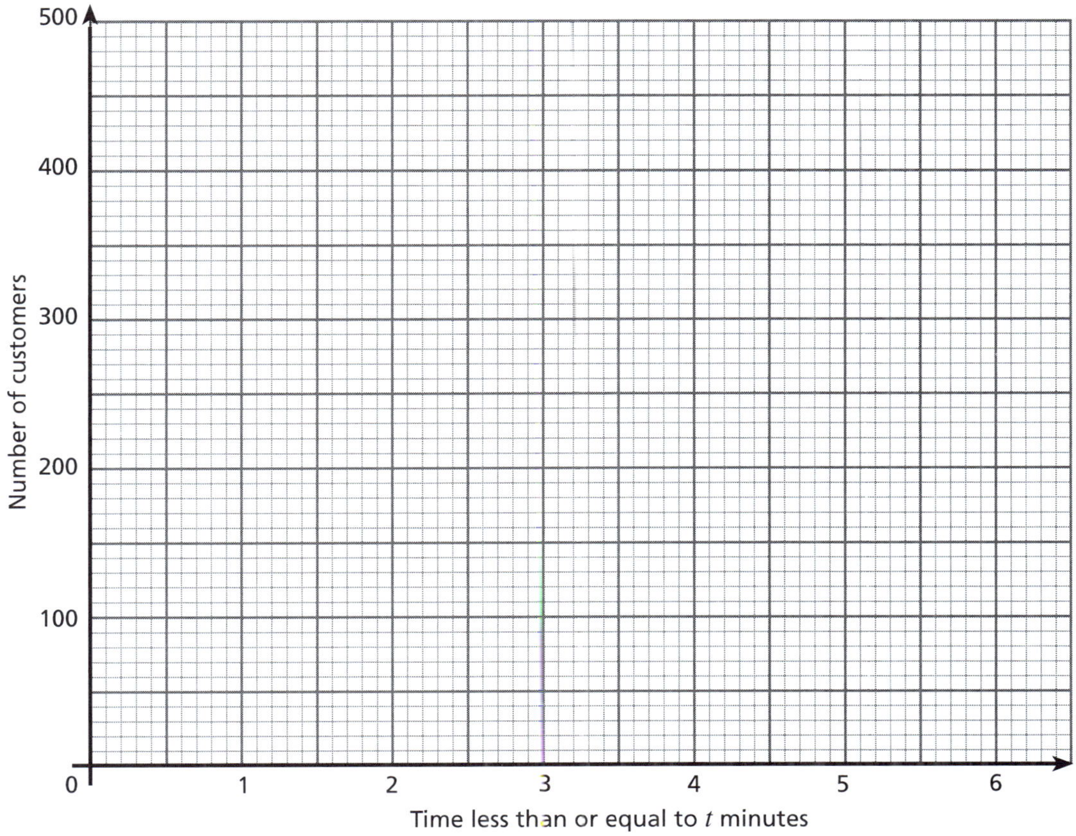

(e) The supermarket is open for $8\frac{1}{2}$ hours on a Saturday and approximately 1000 customers are expected. Use any appropriate average to estimate the number of check-outs which should be used.

....

....

Answer ________________ check-outs

Average used ____________________ (3)

NICCEA 1995

7 A card is selected at random from an ordinary pack of 52 playing cards.

(a) What is the probability of selecting either a red king or a red queen?

....

Answer __________________________ (1)

The pack of cards now has all the jacks, queens and kings removed.

(b) What is the probability of drawing a black six from the remaining cards?

....

Answer __________________________ (1)

QUESTIONS

8 John makes a spinner game for the school fête. When the pointer is spun the probabilities of scoring a colour or a number are given on the table below.

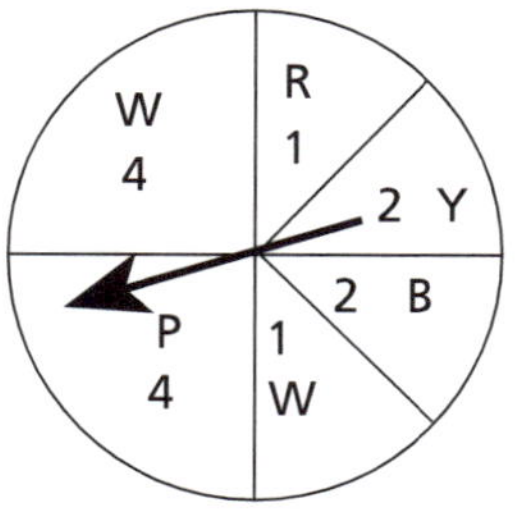

Colour	Probability
white	0.375
purple	0.25
red	0.125
yellow	0.125
blue	0.125

Number	Probability
1	0.25
2	0.25
4	0.5

(a) Find the probability of scoring either a 1 or a 4.

....

Answer ____________________ (2)

(b) Find the probability of getting a purple or a red.

....

Answer ____________________ (2)

(c) Why is the probability of spinning a 1 or a white not 0.25 + 0.375?

.... (3)

9 Little Amy has two spinners, one with four sides, numbered 1, 2, 3, 4 and the other with six sides numbered 1, 2, 3, 4, 5, 6.

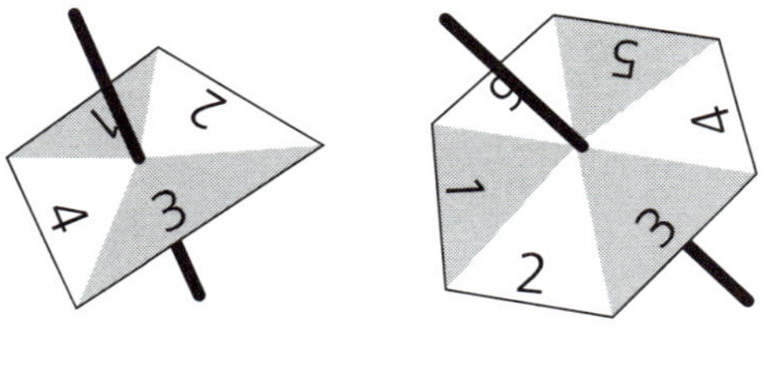

She spins both of them.

(a) List all the possible outcomes.

....

.... (2)

(b) Make a table showing the sum of the two numbers for each outcome.

(2)

QUESTIONS

(c) What is the probability that

(i) the sum is 5, (ii) the sum is odd?

....

Answers: (i) ______________ (1)

(ii) ______________ (1)

Amy's elder brother Richard thinks that the probability of the sum being either 5 or an odd number can be found by adding the two previous answers.

(d) Explain why he is wrong.

.... (1)

(e) How can you work out the probability that the sum is even without using the table?

.... (1)

10 The table shows information about a group of children.

		Boys	Girls
Wears glasses	Yes	5	3
	No	14	10

(a) A boy in the group is chosen at random.
What is the probability that he wears glasses?

....

.... (2)

(b) A child in the group is chosen at random.
The probability that the child wears glasses is 0.25.
What is the probability that the child does **not** wear glasses?

....

.... (1)

SEG 1998

QUESTIONS

11 A pack of 52 playing cards consists of equal numbers of clubs, diamonds, hearts and spades.

Ten cards are removed from the pack and placed face down on a table.

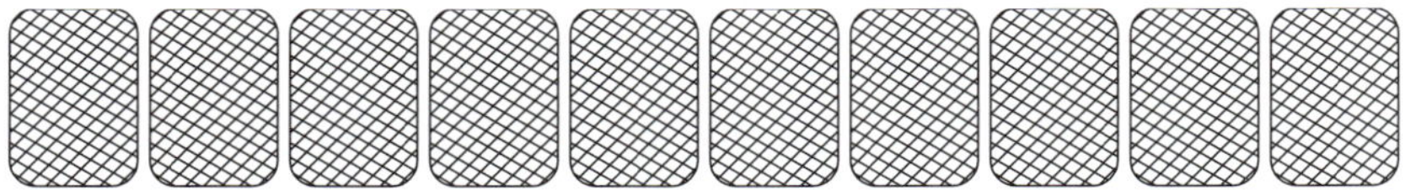

When one of these cards is taken at random the following probabilities apply:

Type of card	Probability
club	0.4
diamond	0.2
heart	0.1
spade	0.3

Number on card	Probability
2	0.2
3	0.2
4	0.1
5	0.3
7	0.2

Four of the ten cards are clubs.

They are numbered 2, 4, 5 and 7.

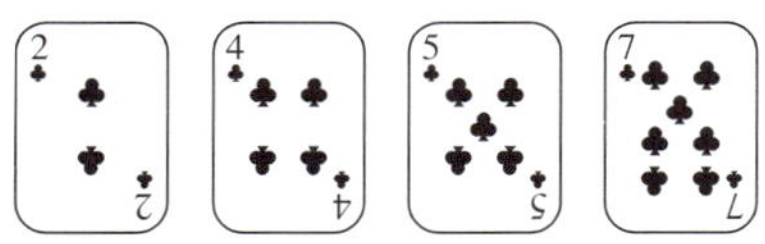

One of the ten cards is taken from the table at random.

(a) What is the probability that it is **not** a diamond?

Answer ______________________ (1)

(b) What is the probability that it is a club or a diamond?

Answer ______________________ (1)

(c) What is the probability that it is a club or numbered 3?

....

Answer ______________________ (2)

(d) Explain why the probability that it is a club or numbered 5 is **not** 0.4 + 0.3.

....

.... (2)

SEG 1995

12 Mr and Mrs Brown plan to have children.
The probability that they have a girl is 0.47.

(a) What is the probability that they have a boy?

.... (1)

(b) Complete the following tree diagram for two children.

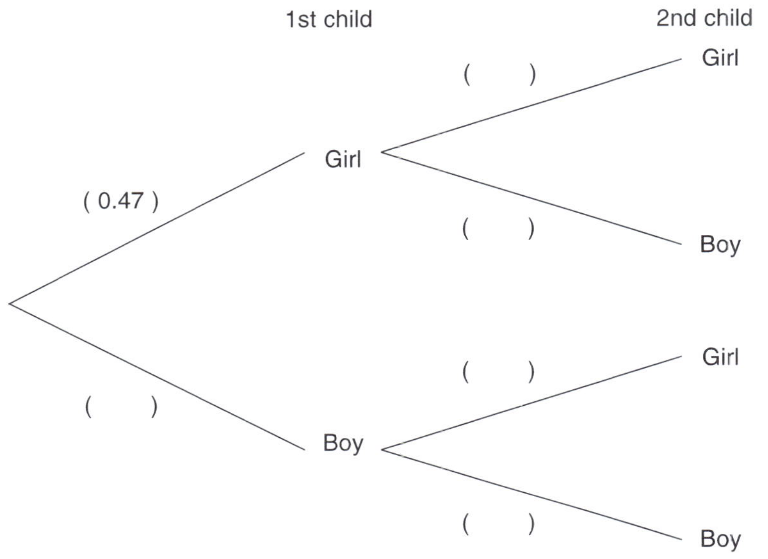

(2)

(c) (i) Find the probability that neither of the two children is a girl.

....

....

.... (3)

(ii) Find the probability that Mr and Mrs Brown have one girl and one boy.
Show your working.

....

....

.... (3)

MEG 1997

5 Mock examination paper

QUESTIONS

Time 2 hours, 100 marks available.

Section A ***Do not use a calculator.***

1 Here is a pattern made with match sticks:

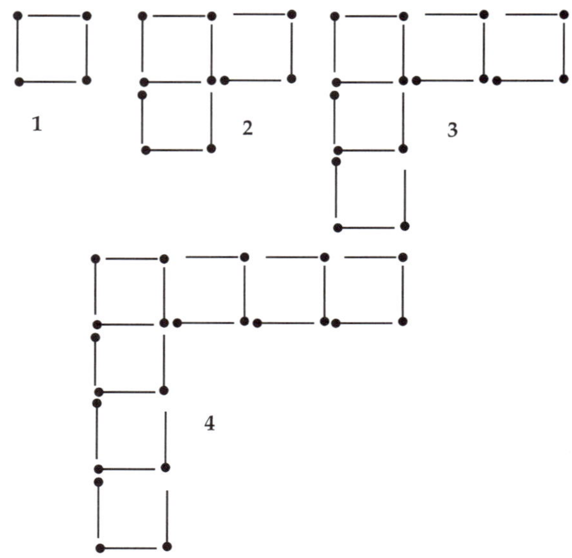

(a) Complete the table:

Pattern number	1	2	3	4	5
Number of squares	1	3	5	7	
Number of matches	4	10			

(2)

(b) Find
  (i) the number of squares; (1)
  (ii) the number of matches (2)
  in pattern 10.

(c) For
  (i) the number of squares and
  (ii) the number of matches
  give the rule for finding the $(n + 1)$th term from the nth term. (2)

(d) Find
  (i) the number of squares and
  (ii) the number of matches
  in pattern n. (3)

2 Here is a recipe for Cheese Straws:

75g flour 40g butter 40g cheese 1 egg 5ml mustard *makes 24 straws*

(a) Mary wants to make 12 cheese straws.
How much cheese should she use? .... (1)

(b) Thomas is making cheese straws for a party. He wants 120.
How much will he need?

.... flour .... butter

.... cheese .... eggs

.... mustard (3)

3 The table shows the lengths and wingspans for some American birds (in inches).

	Length	Wingspan
White Pelican	50	110
Great Cormorant	30	60
Harlequin Duck	12	26
Swallow-tailed Kite	21	50
Bald eagle	32	80
Whooping Crane	45	90
Royal Tern	18	43
Spotted Owl	16	42

(a) Show this information in a scatter graph (2)

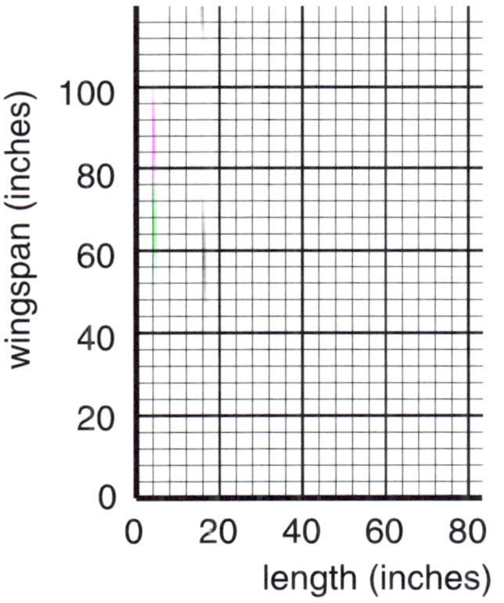

(b) Describe the correlation

.... (1)

(c) (i) draw a line of best fit on your graph (1)

(ii) A Great Blue Heron has a wingspan of 70 inches.
About how long is it?

.... (1)

QUESTIONS

4

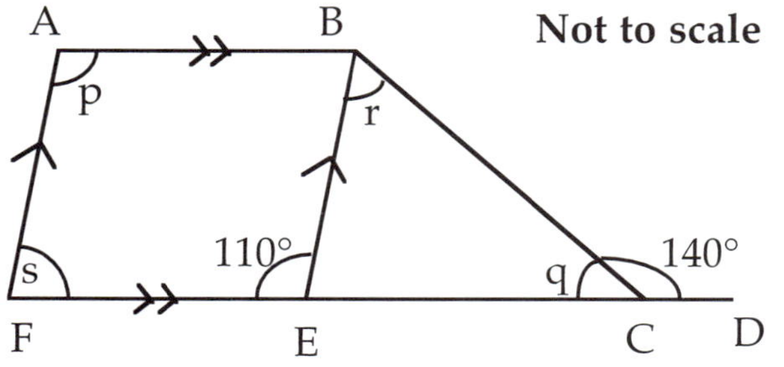

FECD is a straight line

Work out the sizes of the angles marked p, q, r, s.
In each case give a reason for your answer.

p = ... because ....

q = ... because ....

r = ... because ....

s = ... because .... (4)

5 When a drawing pin is dropped on a table, it will either land point up or point down. Joyce and Alex each do an experiment. They use different drawing pins. They drop their drawing pin 10 times and count how many times it lands point up in those 10 drops. They write down this number. They repeat this a number of times, always recording how many times the pin landed point up in each series of 10 drops. Here are their results:

Joyce

4 6 7 3 6 5 4 5 5 7 8 4 7 2 6 3 6 6 5 6

Alex

4 6 4 3 5 2 4 5 4 5

(a) Calculate the median number of point up results for Joyce and Alex.

.... (2)

(b) By calculating the mean number of point up results for Joyce and Alex, estimate the probability of each person's pin landing point up.

.... (3)

(c) Which of the estimated probabilities in part (b) is likely to be the most reliable? Give reasons for your answer.

.... (1)

6 (a) Solve the equations:

(i) $\frac{3x}{4} = 12$ (ii) $2(x-3) = 5x$ (1) + (2)

(iii) $3x + 2 = 4(2 - x)$ (iv) $\frac{x+8}{4} - \frac{x}{3} = \frac{x+5}{6} - \frac{x}{2}$ (2) + (3)

(b) Factorise completely:

(i) $3x^2 - 6xy$ (ii) $x^2 - 7x + 12$ (4)

7 Sam and Ajit are playing a game with these cards:

1	2	3	4	5

They each take one card without looking.

(a) List all the possible outcomes. The first three have been done for you. (2)

Sam	1	2	1
Ajit	2	1	3

(b) What is the probability that

(i) neither card is odd? (1)

(ii) both cards are odd? (1)

(iii) the numbers on the two cards are equal? (1)

(iv) the number on Ajit's card is greater than the number on Sam's card? (1)

8 One solution of the quadratic equation $2x^2 + ax - 6 = 0$, is $x = -2$.

(a) Find the value of a .... (2)

(b) Complete the solution of the equation .... (2)

QUESTIONS

Section B. ***You may use a calculator.***

9 (a) Use your calculator to work out:

$$\frac{27\cdot6\times0\cdot093}{\sqrt{13\cdot69+46\cdot24}}$$

(2)

(b) Show a rough calculation which you can do to check your answer to part (a):

$$\frac{\ldots\ldots\times\ldots\ldots}{\sqrt{\ldots\ldots}}=\ldots\ldots$$

(2)

(c) The value 27·6 was measured correct to the nearest 0·1.
Write down the upper and lower bounds of this measurement.

.... (2)

10 This is a diagram of a metal frame for a stained glass window.

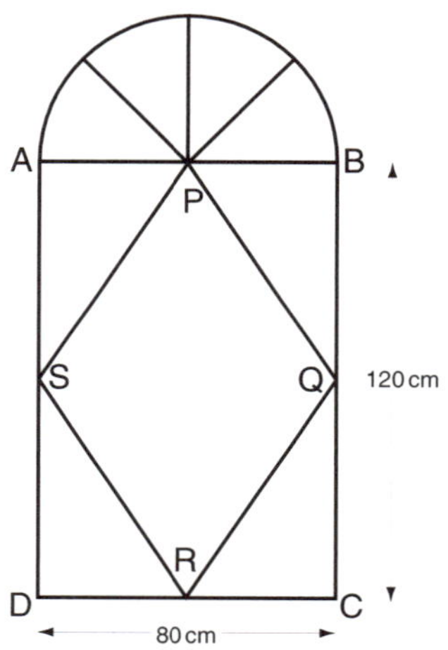

ABCD is a rectangle with a semi-circle mounted on AB.
P, Q, R, S are the mid-points of the sides of the rectangle.
Find the total length of all the pieces of metal needed to make the frame. (8)

11 The glide ratio for a glider is the ratio of vertical distance descended to the horizontal distance covered.

(a) A Kestrel glider has a glide ratio of 13 : 40.
How far does it travel when descending from 4000 m to 1500 m?

.... (2)

(b) A Buzzard glider has a ratio of 0·313. What is the minimum height it must be at for it to land safely at an airfield 10km away?

.... (3)

12 The table shows the weights of a sample of 100 men.

Weight, (x), kg	Frequency
40 ≤ x < 50	2
50 ≤ x ≤ 60	16
60 ≤ x < 70	41
70 ≤ x ≤ 80	27
80 ≤ x < 90	10
90 ≤ x ≤ 100	3
100 ≤ x ≤ 110	1

(a) Calculate an estimate of the mean weight of a man in this sample

.... (3)

(b) (i) Complete the cumulative frequency table for these data;

Weight	<50	<60	<70	<80	<90	<100	<110
Cumulative frequency	2						

(1)

(ii) Draw a cumulative frequency curve. (2)

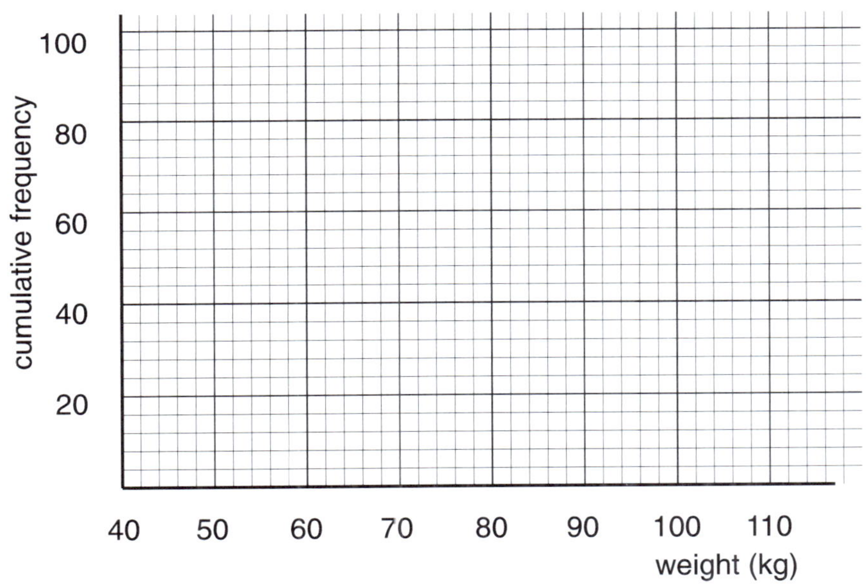

(iii) Use your graph to find the median weight and the interquartile range.

.... (2)

QUESTIONS

13 The distance between Derby and Burton-on-Trent measures 3.7cm on a map. The scale of the map is 1: 500 000. 1 mile = 63 360 inches; 1 inch = 2.54 cm
How far is the actual distance in miles? Give your answer to a sensible degree of accuracy.

.... (3)

14

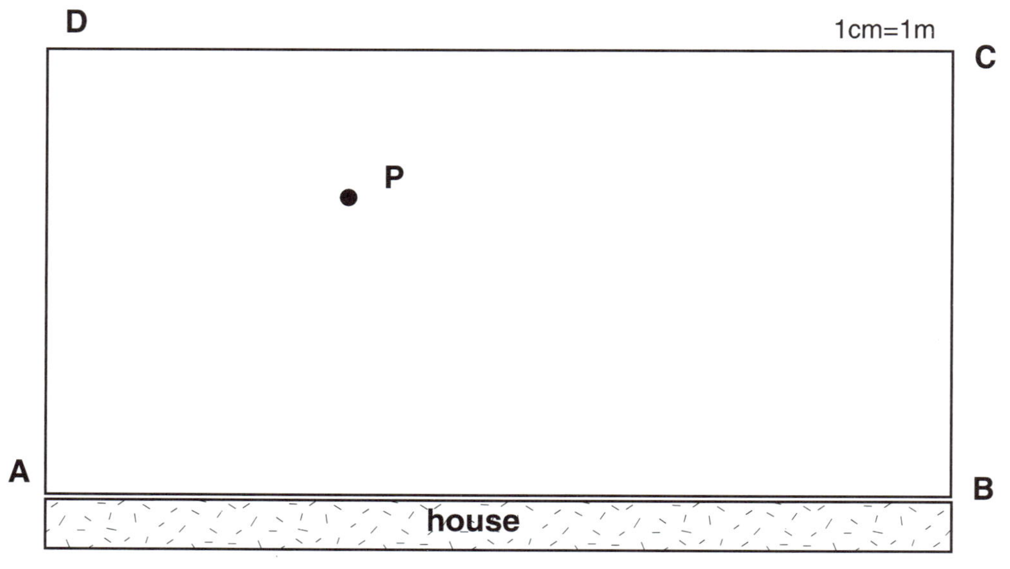

Mark wants to put up a clothes drier. It must be:

- at least 2m from the house
- at least 5m from the tree at P
- the same distance from the fences DC and BC and at least 3m from C

Make an accurate scale drawing to show where the drier can be placed. (4)

15 This formula gives the approximate length of a man's forearm, ($f$cm), when you know his height ($h$cm).

$$h = \frac{10f + 256}{3}$$

(a) An archaeologist found part of a man's skeleton. The forearm was 20 cm long.
How tall was the man? .... (2)

(b) Make f the subject of the formula .... (3)

(c) How long would you expect the forearm of a man 183 cm tall to be? .... (1)

(d) Does the formula work for small children? Explain...

.... (1)

16

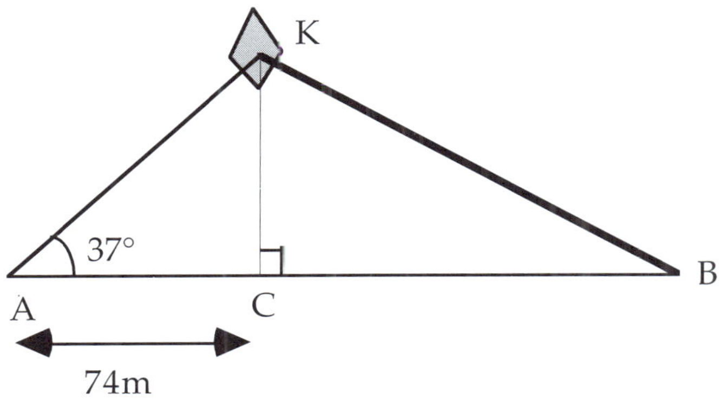

Brian (B) is flying a kite.
Alan (A) measures the distance AC as 74m and the angle KAC as 37°.

(a) How high is the kite? (2)

The length of the string, (BK), is 130m.

(b) What is the angle of elevation of the kite from B? (3)

(c) How far is Brian from Alan? (3)

Answers

1 NUMBER

Question	Answer	Mark
1	$40 \times 7.30 = 292$	1
	$368 \div 36.80 = 10$	1

Examiner's tip It is not necessary to write down the intermediate step but it is a good idea to do so in case you make an error in the second step.

Question	Answer	Mark
2	$\frac{4.5-3.6}{3.6} \times 100$	1
	$= 25\%$	1

Examiner's tip Make sure you use the starting number in the denominator.

Question	Answer	Mark
3	$\frac{5}{7}\times 140$ or $\frac{2}{7}\times 140$	1
	£100 and £40.	1

Examiner's tip Add the two parts of the ratio to find how many parts are required.

Question	Answer	Mark
4	$\frac{12500-12000}{12500}\times 100$	1
	$= 4\%$	1

Examiner's tip In this question the amount was reduced but it is still the starting value that appears under the fraction.

Question	Answer	Mark
5	I increased by 10% means it is multiplied by 1.10	1
	R increased by 20% means it is multiplied by 1.20	1
	$V = IR$ is multiplied by $1.1 \times 1.2 = 1.32$	1
	V is increased by 32%	1

Examiner's tip Using multipliers is the easiest way to tackle this sort of problem.

Question	Answer	Mark
6	$P = \sqrt{\dfrac{4.6 \times 10^6}{2.8 \times 10^2}} = 128.173\,9889$	1
	$= 1.28 \times 10^2$ or 1.3×10^2	1

Examiner's tip Notice that there is a mark for getting the calculation right even if it is not in standard form. Your calculator may not show as many digits as this.

Question	Answer	Mark
7 (a)	5×10^9	1
(b)	$\dfrac{4 \times 10^{11}}{5 \times 10^9}$	1
	$= 8 \times 10$	1

Question	Answer	Mark
8 (a)	(i) 0.021 358 613 (ii) 0.0214 or 0.021	2+1

Examiner's tip This is firstly a test to see if you can use your calculator correctly. A common error is to multiply by 6.81 rather than divide by it. The decision about the answer to (ii), in the absence of other information, is based on the number of figures in each item. In this case two are given to 3 significant figures and it is reasonable to keep to this, or one less, in your answer.

Question	Answer	Mark
(b)	3.9024	2

Examiner's tip This again is to test your ability to use the calculator. It is more efficient to use brackets or the memory than write down an intermediate answer. In all calculator questions it is a good idea to check your answer, either by doing it again, preferably a different way, or by making an estimate to see if your answer is about right.

Question	Answer	Mark
9 (a)	$\dfrac{3}{11}$, 0.3, 33%, $\dfrac{1}{3}$	2
(b) (i)	$\dfrac{12}{15} - \dfrac{10}{15}$	1
	$= \dfrac{2}{15}$	1
(ii)	$\dfrac{6}{7}$	1
(c)	89	2

Examiner's tip There will be one mark if just one number is out of place in part (a). There will also be one mark for a correct attempt to the division in part (c), e.g. 40 × 3827 and 3 × 3827, even if you then made a slip.

Question	Answer	Mark
10 (a)	65	**1**
(b)	67.5, 62.5	**1+1**
(c)	No — the upper bound on the balance is 62.5 which is less than the lower bound on the scales.	**1**
	The scales and the electronic scales could both be right since 65 < 67.5.	**1**
11	$s = \dfrac{25.0^2 - 50.0^2}{2 \times {}^-9.8}$	**2**
	$= 95.7$ or 96 (95.663 265 31)	**1**

Examiner's tip Care needs to be taken with the negative sign when you divide by ⁻9.8, most calculators requiring you to key ± after entering 9.8.

Question	Answer	Mark
12 (a)	$\frac{1}{4} \times 645166$	**1**
	$= 161291.5$	**1**
	$= 161000$	**1**
(b)	$\dfrac{1.04 \times 10^7}{5.80 \times 10^7} \times 100$	**1**
	$= 17.9310\ldots$	**1**
	$= 17.9\%$	**1**

Examiner's tip In each part there is one mark for correct or appropriate accuracy. In part (b) 18% would also be acceptable, but 17.93 would not as the data were only to three significant figures.

Question	Answer	Mark
13	31/12/90: Amount owing = 650 × 1.06 − 243 = £446	**1**
	31/12/91: Amount owing = 446 × 1.06 − 243 = £229.76	**1**
	31/12/92: Amount owing = 229.76 × 1.06 − 243 = £0.55	**1**

Examiner's tip The final answer has been written correct to the nearest penny.

Question	Answer	Mark
14 (a)	84kg	**1**
(b)	170cm	**1**

Question	Answer	Mark
15 (a)	$3 \times 0.8 = 2.4$m	**1**
(b)	$2.4 \times 0.8 = 1.92$m	**1**
(c)	4	**2**

Examiner's tip The easiest way to find the answer to part (c) is to continue multiplying by 0.8 and counting: $3 \times 0.8 = 2.4$ (1); $\times 0.8 = 1.92$ (2); $\times 0.8 = 1.536$ (3); $\times 0.8 = 1.2288$ (4); $\times 0.8 = 0.98304$ (too small).

Question	Answer	Mark
16	8 stones 6 pounds $= 8\frac{6}{14} = 8.428\,571\ldots$ stones	**1**
	Weight in kg $= 8.428\,571 \div 0.157$	**1**
	$= 53.68\ldots = 53.7$	**1+1**
17	Cost $= 1.72 \times 2.2 = £3{\cdot}78$	**1+1**
	Weight $= 10.5 \div (16 \times 2.2) \times 1000 = 298$ g	**1+1**

Examiner's tip You can check your answers by finding $0{\cdot}298 \times 3.78 = 1.127\ldots$ In all cases it is sensible to round to the nearest penny or gram.

2 ALGEBRA

Question	Answer	Mark
1 (a)	$(6 \times 7) + 4$	**1**
(b)	$(8 \times 9) + 6$	**1**
(c)	$(n + 2)(n + 3) + n$	**1**
	$n^2 + 2n + 3n + 6 + n$	**1**
	$n^2 + 6n + 6$	**1**

Examiner's tip 'Simplify your answer' means that you are expected to collect like terms. In this case that means adding together all the n terms.

Question	Answer	Mark
2 (a) (i)	38, 51	**1**
(ii)	The differences between terms are successive odd numbers, so the next term will be 51 + the next odd number, 15.	**1**

Question			Answer	Mark
	(b)	(i)	n^2	1
		(ii)	Each term is 2 more than the term in the sequence in (b)(i).	1
			$n^2 + 2$	1

Examiner's tip You can find this nth term using the differences noted in part (a) but the question has been arranged to help you spot the connection between the sequence and the more familiar square numbers.

Question			Answer	Mark
3	(a)	(i)	$\sqrt{(10^2+24^2)}$	1
			$= 26$	1
		(ii)	$\sqrt{(12^2+35^2)}$	1
			$= 37$	1
	(b)	(i)	22	1
		(ii)	48	1
	(c)	(i)	$2 + 2n$ or $2(n + 1)$	2
		(ii)	If $n = 1$, $1^2 + k = 3$, $k = 2$	1

Examiner's tip Notice that sequence p is the even numbers but not starting with 2. This gives a clue to finding the nth term. In part (c)(ii), you can use any value of n to find k. For example, $n = 5$, $25 + 5k = 35$ also gives $k = 2$.

Question			Answer	Mark
4	(a)		$6x^2 + 21x - 12x - 42$	1
			$6x^2 + 9x - 42$	1
	(b)	(i)	$(x + 3)(x - 2)$	2

Examiner's tip The '$+x$' in the expression means that it will be '+3' and '−2' in the brackets.

Question			Answer	Mark
		(ii)	$x = {}^{-}3$ or $x = 2$	1+1

Question			Answer	Mark
5			$2x - 3 + 2(x + 2) = 15$	1
			$2x - 3 + 2x + 4 = 15$	1
			$4x = 14$	1
			$x = 3\frac{1}{2}$	1

Examiner's tip As it is an equation, you can multiply both sides by the common denominator, which is 6.

Question	Answer	Mark
6 (a)	$3n - 4 < 17$	1
(b)	$3n < 17 + 4$	1
	$n < 7$	1

Examiner's tip Although solving this inequality looks much the same as solving the equation $3n - 4 = 18$, it is important to keep the inequality sign the right way round. In some cases this will not be so obvious.

Question	Answer	Mark
7 (a)	Graphs drawn (see below) $y = 2x - 2$	2
	$y = 3 - x$	1

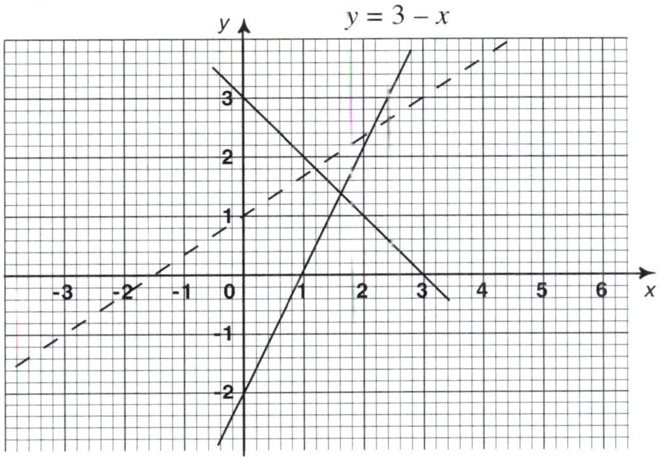

Question	Answer	Mark
(b)	$x = 1.2, y = 1.8$	1

Examiner's tip The first graph earns 2 marks, one for the correct gradient. Take care in reading the scales as one small square is 0.2.

Question	Answer	Mark
8	$2x + 3y = 17$ ....(i)	
	$3x - 2y = 6$.................(ii) number the equations for identification	
	(i) times 3 gives $6x + 9y = 51$ ....(iii)	
	(ii) times 2 gives $6x - 4y = 12$ ....(iv)	
	subtract: $13y = 39$	1
	therefore $y = 3$	1
	substitute in (i) gives: $2x + 9 = 17$	1
	$2x = 8$	
	$x = 4$	1

Examiner's tip Note an alternative method would be to multiply (i) by 2 and (ii) by 3 and to find x by adding the new equations.

Question	Answer	Mark
9	$s = 10 \times 11 \times 21 \div 6$	1
	$= 385$	1

Question	Answer		Mark
10 (a)	$Q = 3600 \times 12 \times 2 \div 55$		**1**
	$= 1570(.909\ldots)$		**1**

Examiner's tip An answer of 1570 is reasonable here but not 1600, since the capacity is not as big as this.

Question	Answer		Mark
(b)	$1000 = 3600 \times 15 \times N \div 120$		**1**
	$N = 1000 \times 120 \div 3600 \div 15$		**1**
	$= 2.2\ldots$, i.e. 3 lanes.		**1**

Examiner's tip You might prefer to attempt this part another way, by changing the formula first, so that N is the subject. This formula would be: $N = \dfrac{QC}{3600V}$.

Question	Answer		Mark
11	$F = 2C$		**1**
	$C = \frac{5}{9}(2C - 32)$	(substituting for F)	**1**
	$9C = 10C - 160$	(multiplying by 9 and expanding the bracket)	**1**
	$-C = -160$	(subtracting $10C$ from both sides)	
	$C = 160$		**1**
12	Mean $= (30 + 40 + x + 50 + 80) \div 5 = 40 + \dfrac{x}{5}$		**1**
	Median $= x$		**1**
	$40 + \dfrac{x}{5} = x$		**1**
	$\dfrac{4}{5}x = 40$	(subtracting $\dfrac{x}{5}$ from both sides)	**1**
	$x = 50$	(multiplying by 5 and dividing by 4)	**1**
13 (a)	$3d + 7w = 53.4$		**1**
	$d + 10w = 50$		**1**
(b)	$3d + 30w = 150$	(multiplying second equation by 3)	**1**
	$3d + 7w = 53.4$	(first equation)	
	$23w = 96.6$	(subtracting the equations)	**1**
	$w = 4.2$	(dividing by 23)	**1**
	$d = 50 - 10 \times 4.2 = 8$	(substituting in second equation)	**1**
14	0, 1, 2, 3		**2**

Examiner's tip Notice that $^-1$ is not included as the numbers must be greater than it. However 3 is included as that inequality sign includes 'equals'.

Question	Answer		Mark
15 (a)	$3x = 14, x = 4\frac{2}{3}$		1 + 1
(b)	$2x - 1 = 7, 2x = 8$		1
	$x = 4$		1
(c)	$6x + 3 = 18, 6x = 15$		1
	$x = 2\frac{1}{2}$		1

Examiner's tip There are other ways to solve such equations, e.g., in part (b), multiply out the bracket: $10x - 5 = 35$, $10x = 40$.

Question	Answer		Mark
16	$20 = \sqrt{\dfrac{2 \times 3950 \times h}{5280}}$		1
	$h = \dfrac{20^2 \times 5280}{2 \times 3950} = 267(.34...)$		1+1

Examiner's tip You could also rearrange the formula before substituting. The formula would be

$$h = \frac{5280D^2}{2r}$$

Question	Answer		Mark
17	$PV = k$	(multiplying both sides by V)	1
	$V = \dfrac{k}{P}$	(dividing both sides by P)	1

Examiner's tip It is safer to do this in two simple steps.

Question	Answer		Mark
18 (a)	$2x \leqslant 15$	(adding 7 to both sides)	
	$x \leqslant 7\frac{1}{2}$	(dividing both sides by 2)	1
(b)	$^-x > {}^-1$	(subtracting 3 from both sides)	
	$x < 1$	(dividing both sides by $^-1$ and changing sign)	1

Examiner's tip It is important to notice that if you change the signs of the two sides of an inequality, in this case from negative to positive, it is necessary to change the inequality sign also. For example, $7 > 4$ but $^-7 < {}^-4$.
You can do it another way:

$3 > 2 + x$	(adding x to both sides)
$1 > x$	(subtracting 2 from both sides)
$x < 1$	(writing from right to left)

Question	Answer		Mark
(c)	$x^2 < 4$	(subtracting 4 from both sides)	
	If $x > 0, x < 2$	(taking positive square root)	1
	If $x < 0, x > {}^-2$	(taking negative square root and therefore changing inequality sign)	1

Examiner's tip These two inequalities can be combined as $^-2 < x < 2$.

Question	Answer	Mark
19	$x = 2.5$ gives 3.125	
	$x = 2.75$ gives 7.046	1
	$x = 2.9$ gives 9.889	
	$x = 2.8$ gives 7.952	1
	$x = 2.85$ gives 8.8991	
	$x = 2.86$ gives 9.09…	1
	$x = 2.855$ gives 8.996…	
	Solution $x = 2.86$ (to two decimal places)	1

Examiner's tip As $x = 2.855$ gives a value which is less than 9, the solution must be greater than 2.855, i.e., 2.86 rather than 2.85. Remember that it is the value of x which is required to two decimal places, not the value of the expression $x^3 - 5x$.

Question	Answer		Mark
20 (a)	Area $= y^2 - 4 \times \frac{1}{2}x^2$		1
	$= y^2 - 2x^2$		1
(b)	$x^2 + x^2 = 14^2$	(applying Pythagoras to any corner triangle)	1
	$2x^2 = 196$		
	$x^2 = 98$		1
	$x = 9.899...$		1

Examiner's tip Although not a sensible degree of accuracy for a practical problem, keep all the figures on your calculator for the next calculations.

Question	Answer	Mark
(c)	$y = 14 + 2x = 33.798...$	1
	Area $= 33.798^2 - 2 \times 9.899^2$	
	$= 946\,\text{cm}^2$	1

Examiner's tip In this case, had you used the rounded answers $x = 9.0$ and $y = 33.8$ you would have still obtained the above answer but that is not always so – only round at the end.

Question	Answer	Mark
21 (a) (i)	lines drawn as shown, 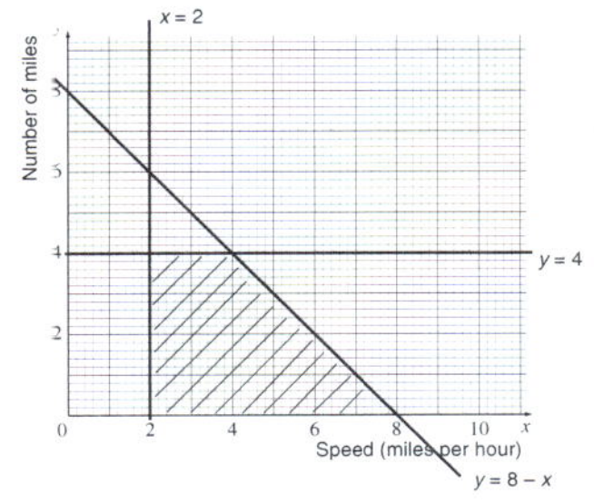	**3**
(ii)	correct shading	**3**
(b) (i)	$2x = -6$	**1**
	$x = -3$	**1**
(ii)	$x \geqslant -3$	**1**

Examiner's tip Take care with the ≤ sign in (b)(ii). When solving the equation you find $5 - 11 = 2x$, so the inequality is $-6 \leq 2x$, or $x \geq -3$

Question	Answer	Mark
22	A: Cycling at constant speed	**1**
	B: Slowing down (going uphill)	**1**
	C: Accelerating (going downhill)	**1**
	D: Maximum speed (bottom of hill)	**1**

Examiner's tip Do not be deceived into thinking that when the graph goes up it is a hill! It actually means the cyclist is going faster, so it is more likely to be down a hill.

Question	Answer	Mark
23 (a)	80 seconds	**1**
(b)	10 metres	**1**
(c)	Robert – steeper graph	**1**

---

24 (a) and (b)

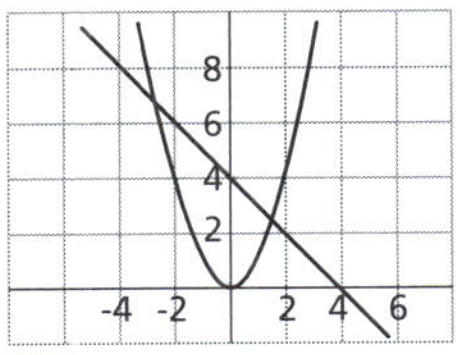

Straight line **1**
Curve **2**

(c) (i) 1.6, $^-2.6$ **1+1**

Examiner's tip You cannot read a hand-drawn graph more accurately than this.

(ii) $x =$	$x^2 + x - 4 =$	
1.6	0.16	
1.55	– 0.0475	
1.57	0.0349	
1.56	– 0.0064	**1**
1.56 is closer		**1**

Question	Answer		Mark
	− 2.6	0.16	
	− 2.5	− 0.25	
	− 2.57	0.0349	
	− 2.56	− 0.0064	1
	− 2.56 is closer		1

Examiner's tip You should not need many trials as the starting point was quite accurate.

---

25 (a) and (b)

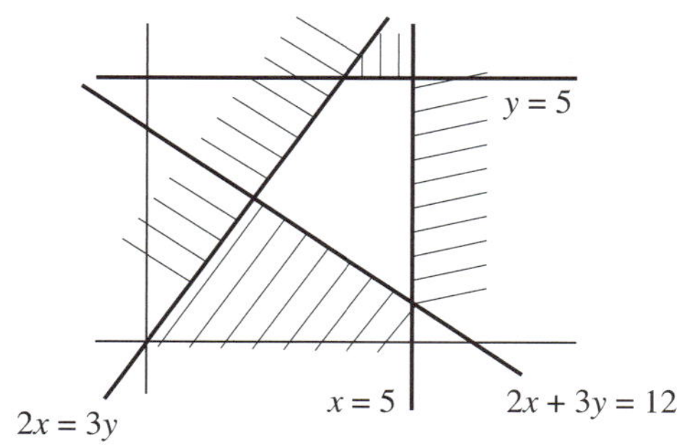

4

Examiner's tip If you shade the regions which are **not** included it will be easier to look for possible solution points, should they be asked for.

26

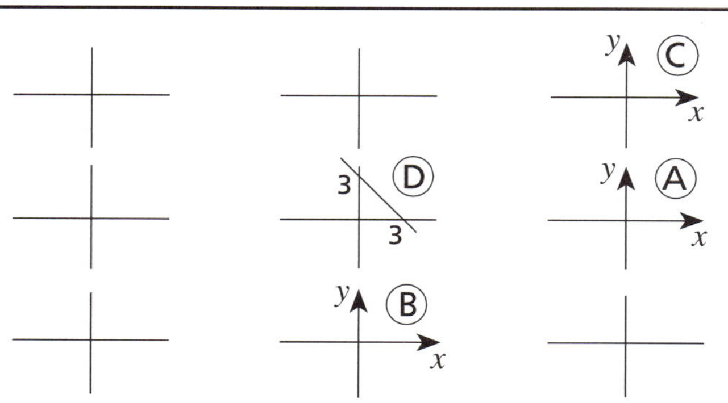

Marks: 1, 1+1, 1

---

27 (a) Area of square $= x^2$ 1

Area of triangle $= \frac{1}{2} \times 0.5 \times x$ 1

Total area $= x^2 + \frac{1}{4}x$ 1

(b) Volume $= 4x \times \text{area}$ 1

$= 4x^3 + x^2$ 1

So $4x^3 + x^2 = 10$ 1

Letts Q&A

Question	Answer		Mark
(c)	$x = 1$	$4x^3 + x^2 = 5$	
	$x = 2$	$4x^3 + x^2 = 36$	1
	$x = 1.5$	$4x^3 + x^2 = 15.75$	
	$x = 1.25$	$4x^3 + x^2 = 9.375$	1
	$x = 1.3$	$4x^3 + x^2 = 10.478$	1
	Result 1.3		1

Examiner's tip If greater accuracy were required in part (c), the next step would be to find the value when $x = 1.275$ and 1.28.

Question	Answer	Mark
28 (a)	$3x^2 - 4x + 6x - 8$	
	$= 3x^2 + 2x - 8$	2
(b)	$5b\,(a + 2b)$	2
(c)	$c + 4d = 2a$	
	$4d = 2a - c$	
	$d = \dfrac{2a - c}{4}$	2

Examiner's tip In (c) make *d* positive by adding it to both sides first. Show all three steps in working

3 SHAPE, SPACE AND MEASURES

Question	Answer	Mark
1 (a)	Area of triangle $ABC = \frac{1}{2} \times 3 \times 4$	1
	Volume of prism = 2 × area of triangle	1
	= 12	1
	m^3 or cubic metres	1
(b)	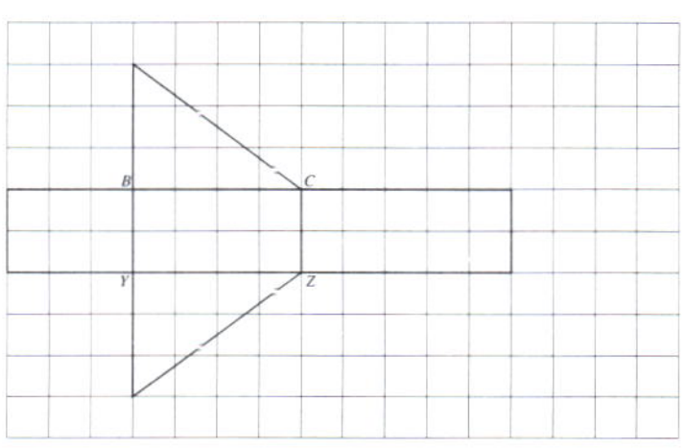	
	Rectangles	1 + 1
	Triangles	1

Examiner's tip Other arrangements of the net are possible, but the only others that will fit in the space have the triangles attached to the rectangle on the left or, more awkwardly, the right.

Question	Answer	Mark
2 (a)	Radius $= \frac{1}{2} \times (4 + 6)$	1
	$= 5$	1
(b)	Area $= \pi \times 2^2 + \pi \times 3^2$	2
	$= 40.8$	1

Examiner's tip You will have to remember the formula for the area of a circle, πr^2

Question	Answer	Mark
3	Area of rectangle $= 6 \times 12$	1
	$= 72$	1
	Area of circles $= 2 \times \pi \times 3^2$	1
	$= 56.5\ldots$	1
	Area left $= 72 - 56.5\ldots = 15.45$ or 15.5	1

Examiner's tip You do not need to write down the intermediate answers but it is wise to show how you did the calculation in case you make an error. The marks for your method could still be given.

Question	Answer	Mark
4	The pool is a prism whose cross section is a trapezium.	1
	Area of cross section $= \frac{1}{2} \times 25 \times (2 + 4)$	1
	$= 75$	1
	Volume $= 15 \times 75 = 1125$	1

Examiner's tip The top edge of the pool is horizontal and the sides vertical, so the diagram shows the cross section:

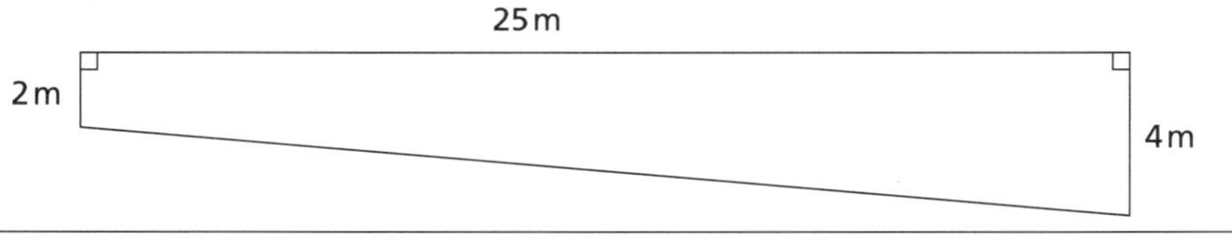

Question	Answer	Mark
5 (a)	Use of $\frac{12}{10}$	1
	$\frac{12}{10}$	
	$= 14.4$ cm	1

Examiner's tip It is important to identify which are the corresponding sides. *OC* corresponds to *OB* and *CD* corresponds to *AB*. If in doubt about which way up the multiplier (scale factor) should be, notice that *CD* is in the larger triangle.

Question	Answer	Mark
6	Circumference of two inner semicircles $= 400 - 2 \times 90 = 220$	1
	Radius of inner semicircles $= 220 \div 2\pi = 35.014\ldots$	1
	Radius of outer semicircles $= 8 + 35.014\ldots = 43.014\ldots$	1
	Circumference of two outer semicircles $= 2 \times \pi \times 43.014 = 270$	1
	Extra distance $= 270 - 220 = 50$	1

Examiner's tip You will need to remember the formula for the circumference of a circle. Notice that the 'straights' are all 90 m long. An answer given to the nearest metre is reasonable in this practical situation.

Question	Answer	Mark
7 (a)	Volume $= \pi \times 1.5^2 \times 14.5$	1
	$= 102.4944\ldots$	1
(b)	Volume of toothpaste 'cylinder' $= \pi \times 3.5^2 \times 15\,\text{mm}^3$	1
	$1\,\text{cm}^3 = 1000\,\text{mm}^3$	1
	Number of times $= \dfrac{\pi \times 1.5^2 \times 14.5 \times 1000}{\pi \times 3.5^2 \times 15}$	1
	$= 177$	1

Examiner's tip Don't forget the change of units in part (b). It would not be reasonable to round up the final answer as part of a 'cylinder' is not enough to clean my teeth. In fact the situation is actually more approximate, since toothpaste tubes are not cylinders, but the wording of the question tells you to take it as a cylinder.

Question	Answer	Mark
8	$\tan x = \dfrac{5.2}{4.35}$	1+1
	$x = 50.08\ldots$	1
	$= 50.1$ or 50	1

Examiner's tip Take care you show how you did the calculation, even though it was all done on the calculator. It is sensible not to leave too many figures in the answer in this practical situation.

Question	Answer	Mark
9 (a)	$? = \sqrt{14^2 + 8^2}$	2
	$= 16.12\ldots$	1

Examiner's tip This is the easiest case when using Pythagoras.

Question	Answer	Mark
(b)	$? = \sqrt{7^2 - 6^2}$	2
	$= 3.6055\ldots$	1

Letts Q&A

Question	Answer	Mark

Examiner's tip This is the rearranged form, deriving from $7^2 = 6^2 + ?^2$. This question is not set in a practical context so the number of digits in your answer is not important, so long as there are enough to show you have done it correctly, e.g., 16.1 and 3.61 would be perfectly acceptable.

Question	Answer	Mark
10 (a)	$5.50 \sin 70° = 5.168\ldots$	**2**
	$= 5.17$	**1**
(b)	$5.50 \cos 70° = 1.881\ldots$	**2**
	$= 1.88$	**1**

Examiner's tip You need to realise that the angle to use is on the safety notice, since 'how far **can** it reach' implies maximum angle, which is 70°.

Question	Answer	Mark
(c)	$1.8 \tan 67°$	**2**
	$= 4.24$	**1**

Examiner's tip It is reasonable to give 2 decimal places in your answers since this was the accuracy of the data.

Question	Answer	Mark
11 (a)	$2\pi \times 68 = 427.2\ldots$	**1**
	$427.2 \div 4 = 106.8\ldots$	**1**
	$= 107$ (to 3 significant figures)	**1**

(b)

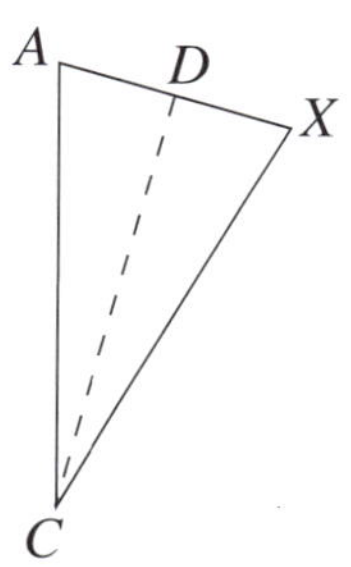

Answer	Mark
Angle $ACD = \frac{1}{2} \times 30 = 15°$	**1**
$AD = 68 \sin 15°$	**1**
$= 17.5\ldots$	**1**
$AX = 2 \times AD = 35$ (2 s.f.)	**1**

Examiner's tip You need to remember the formula for the circumference of a circle in part (a) and realise that the triangle ACX is isosceles to start the solution to part (b).

Question	Answer	Mark
12 (a)	$\frac{1}{2} \times 5 \times (6 + 11) = 42 \cdot 5$	**2**
(b) (i)	$11 \cdot 46$	**3**

Question	Answer	Mark
(ii)	$\approx \frac{2\times 50}{4+5}$	
	$= \frac{100}{9}$	1+1+1
(c) (i)	AD2 = 2·52 + 3·82 = 20·69	1+1
	AD = √20·69 = 4.55	1
(ii)	EC = 18 − 12 − 2.5 = 3.5	1
(iii)	tan (angle BCE) = $\frac{3.8}{3.5}$	2
	angle BCE = 47.4°	1

Examiner's tip In part (b), use the brackets on your calculator for the 3.61 + 5.23. There is one mark in part (c)(iii) for recognising that you need to use the tangent to find the angle.

Question	Answer	Mark
13 (a)	$PR^2 = 1.4^2 + 2.6^2$	1
	$PR = \sqrt{(1.4^2+2.6^2)}$	1
	= 2.95	1
(b)	X is true	1

Examiner's tip You must show how you are using Pythagoras as well as obtaining the length. In part (b), imagine that PS and SR are rods hinged at S. If angle PSR increases then PR also increases.

Question	Answer		Mark
14 (a)	$\tan 75° = \frac{AD}{2.4}$		1
	$AD = 2.4 \times \tan 75°$		1
	= 8.96		1
(b)	$\sin x = \frac{8.96}{14.4}$		1+1
	$x = 38.5°$		1
(c)	$FC = 1.8 \tan 75°$	$\frac{FC}{AD} = \frac{1.8}{2.4}$	1
		$FC = AD \times \frac{1.8}{2.4}$	1
	= 6.72		1

Examiner's tip You would score full marks in part (c) for correctly multiplying your answer to part (a) by 0.75 i.e. $\frac{1.8}{2.4}$.

Question	Answer	Mark
15 (a)	146°	**1**

Examiner's tip If in doubt, sketch a diagram.

(b)	Average gradient $= \dfrac{293 - 150}{500}$	**1**
	$= 0.286$	**1**

Examiner's tip Don't forget to make the units the same.

16 (a)	$\dfrac{AD}{4.5} = \cos 26°$	**1**
	$AD = 4.5\cos 26°$	**1**
	$= 4.04$	**1**
(b)	$\sin ABD = \dfrac{4.0445\ldots}{4.2}$	**1**
	$ABD = 74.4°$	**1**

Examiner's tip Although it is sensible to give the answer to part (a) to no more than three significant figures, do not use this rounded answer in working out part (b).

Keep all the figures in your calculator and divide by 4.2. (If you use $\dfrac{4.04}{4.2}$, you will get 74.1° as the answer to (b).

17	$2\pi rk$, $2\pi r^2$. These could both be areas as they involve length × length.	**1**
	The others involve length × length × length and could be volumes.	**1**

18 (a)

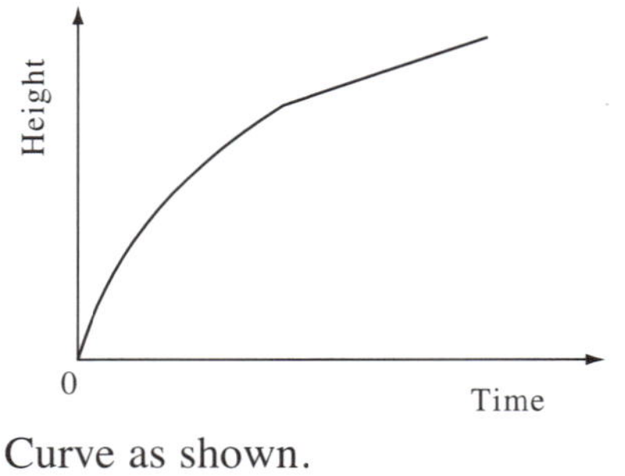

	Curve as shown.	**1**
	Straight line as shown.	**1**
(b)	$\frac{1}{2}(a + b)c$	**1**

Question			Answer	Mark
19	(a)	(i)	$\frac{1}{2} \times \pi \times 0.8$	**1**
			$= 1.26$	**1**
		(ii)	$1.26 + 0.8 + 2 \times 2.2$	
			$= 6.46$	**1**
	(b)	(i)	$AE^2 = 5^2 - 2.2^2$	**1**
			$AE = \sqrt{(5^2 - 2.2^2)}$	**1**
			$= 4.49$	**1**
		(ii)	$DE = 2\cos 50°$	**1**
			$= 1.29$	**1**

Examiner's tip Don't forget to write down your methods as these earn most of the marks.

Question			Answer	Mark
20	(a)		$ABQP$ is a parallelogram so AB remains parallel to PQ, which is horizontal	**1**
	(b)	(i)	B moves on an arc of a circle radius QB	**1**
		(ii)	X moves on an arc of equal size at a distance XB above B	**1**
	(c)		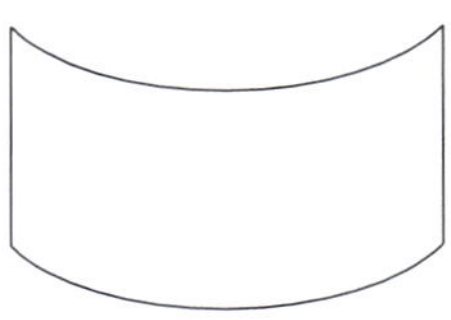	**2**

Question			Answer	Mark
21	(a)	(i)	straight line perpendicular to GS through mid point of GS	**1+1**
		(ii)	Arc of circle centre W radius 10 cm	**1+1**
		(iii)	Part of line indicated as in diagram.	1
			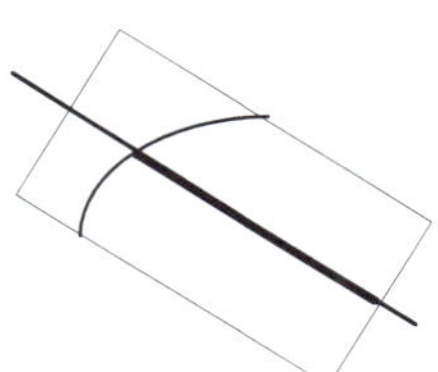	
	(b)	(i)	scale factor = 20 ÷ 8 = 2.5	**1+1**
		(ii)	w = 7.5 ÷ 2.5 = 3	**1+1**

Examiner's tip Do this as accurately as you can – don't forget the compasses to draw the arc!

4 HANDLING DATA

Question	Answer	Mark

1 (a) and (b)

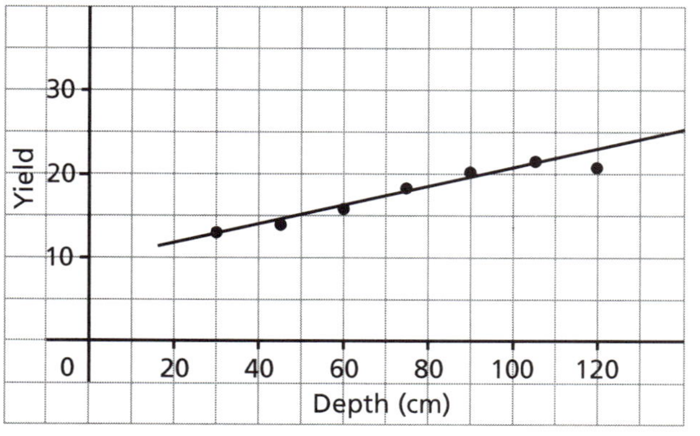

Plotting points **2**
Line **1**

(c) Reading from graph at 100 cm **1**

(d) It is beyond the last depth so we do not know what would happen. **1**
The last reading is lower than the one before it. **1**

Examiner's tip Your line of best fit should ideally leave as many points above the line as below it all the way along.

---

2 (a) Mean = £23 562.50 **1**
Median = £22 250 **1**
Mode = £19 000 **1**

(b) The mode – it is the lowest salary paid. **1**

Examiner's tip The median is halfway between the two middle values when they are ranked.

---

3 (a) **3**

Name	Age	Sex	Cereal	Juice	Fruit	Bread	Cooked
J Smith	16	B	✓	✓	✗	✗	✗
J Jones	17	G	✗	✗	✗	✗	✗

(b) **1** Did you eat any fruit today? **1**

2 Did you eat any vegetables today? **1**

3 Did you eat any chips today? **1**

Examiner's tip Your observation sheet may be very different but it must offer the opportunity to draw various conclusions, having worked out statistics based on the answers to your questions. It is important in part (b) to fix a definite time. You must be able to separate fruit, vegetables and chips to check the statements.

Question	Answer	Mark
4 (a) (i)	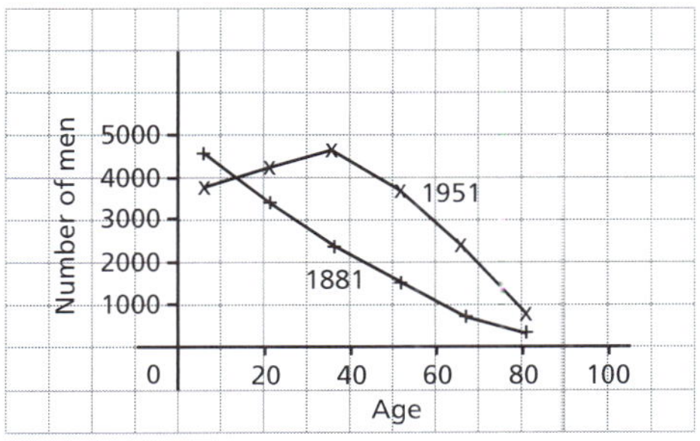	4 (1 mark deducted for each mistake)
(ii)	Mean (1881) = (7.5 × 4740 + 22.5 × 3380 + etc.) ÷ 12 620	1
	= 26.0 years	1
	Mean (1951) = (7.5 × 3785 + etc.) ÷ 19 062	1
	= 36.0 years	1

Examiner's tip If your calculator will do statistics, learn how to use it – it is much quicker! However, do it twice as a check.

Question	Answer	Mark
(iii)	More men in 1951	1
	Higher average age in 1951	1

Examiner's tip You will also be given credit for other relevant comments, e.g. 'Men lived longer in 1951', 'There were more men over 60 in 1951', etc.

(b) (i)

Cumulative frequencies:	1881	1951
under 15	4740	3785
under 30	8120	7935
under 45	10370	12574
under 60	11800	16296
under 75	12510	18528
under 90	12620	19062

1–1

(ii)

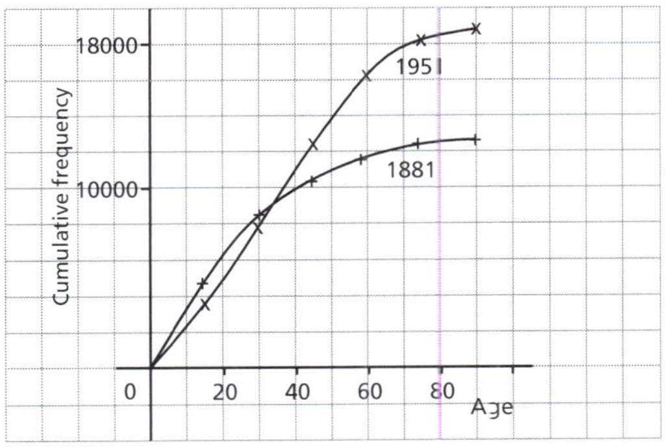

2–2

(1 mark deducted for each mistake)

Question	Answer	Mark

(c)

	Median	IQ range	% over 21	
1881	20	38 − 10 = 28	50	1+1+1
1951	35	50 − 20 = 30	73	1+1+1

Examiner's tip Read medians at half total frequency (6310/9531). Read quartiles at 25%/75% of total frequency (3155/9465, 4765/14 296). Subtract readings at 21 years from total frequency and convert to percentages.

(d) Fewer young men in 1951 (% under 21) **1**
Greater spread of ages (interquartile range greater) in 1951 **1**

Examiner's tip There are other possible comments but make sure yours are different from the earlier part.

---

5 (a)

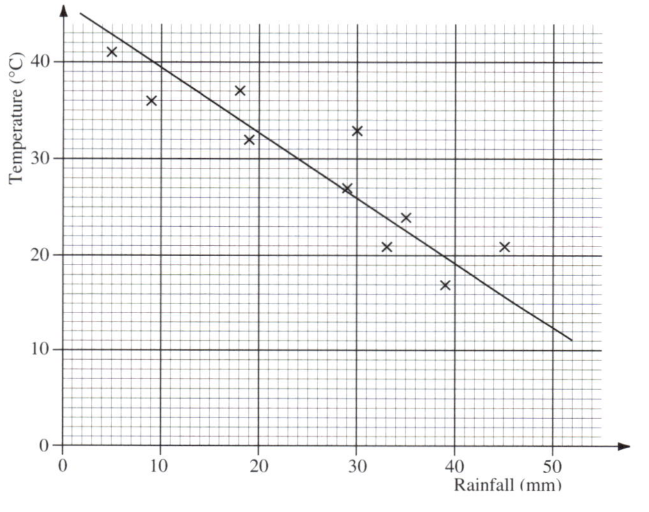

2

(b) (Strong) negative correlation. **1**

(c) Line drawn on graph. **1**

(d) About 25 mm. **1**

Examiner's tip There is 1 mark in part (a) if you plotted a point wrongly. The negative correlation is quite strong. The answer to part (d) should be the reading from your graph.

---

6 (a) Mean = (0.5 × 83 + 1.5 × 138 + 2.5 × 141 + 3.5 × 68 +
4.5 × 45 + 5.5 × 25) ÷ 500 **1+1**
= 1179 ÷ 500 **1**
= 2.358 **1**

(b) (83) 221 362 430 475 500 **3**

Question		Answer	Mark
(c)		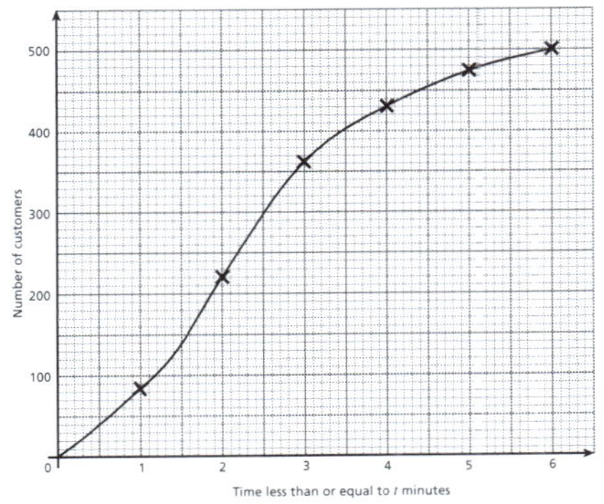	4
(d)	(i)	2.2 minutes	1
	(ii)	3.1 − 1.4	1
		= 1.7 minutes	1
(e)		Mode is 2.5	1
		Average number = (Average time × 1000) ÷ 510	1
		(with mode) = 4.9	
		Needs 5 checkouts	1

Examiner's tip In parts (b) and (c) you will lose marks for errors. Remember to show what you are calculating, even though you use your calculator. In part (e) you could argue for using any average but the mode does make allowance for any peak in the numbers.

Question		Answer	Mark
7	(a)	$\frac{4}{52} = \frac{1}{13}$ (b) $\frac{2}{40} = \frac{1}{20}$	1+1

Examiner's tip Decimal answers are also acceptable, but not ratios or statements such as '1 out of 13'.

Question		Answer	Mark
8	(a)	0.25 + 0.5 = 0.75	2
	(b)	0.25 + 0.125 = 0.375	2
	(c)	One section contains white and 1.	1
		The probability for white and 1 has been added in twice.	2

Examiner's tip The condition that needs to be satisfied before probabilities can be added is sometimes referred to as the outcomes being 'mutually exclusive'.

Question		Answer	Mark
9	(a)	1,1; 1,2; 1,3; 1,4; 1,5; 1,6; 2,1; 2,2; 2,3; 2,4; 2,5; 2,6; 3,1; 3,2; 3,3; 3,4; 3,5; 3,6; 4,1; 4,2; 4,3; 4,4; 4,5; 4,6.	2

Examiner's tip The order is important. 1 on the first and 2 on the second is a different outcome from 2 on the first and 1 on the second.

Question	Answer	Mark

(b)

	1	2	3	4	5	6
1	2	3	4	5	6	7
2	3	4	5	6	7	8
3	4	5	6	7	8	9
4	5	6	7	8	9	10

2

(c) (i) $\frac{1}{6}$ (ii) $\frac{12}{24} = \frac{1}{2}$ **1 + 1**

(d) 5 is also an odd number so the outcomes are not mutually exclusive. **1**

(e) If the sum is even it is not odd so the probability is $1 - \frac{1}{2} = \frac{1}{2}$ **1**

Examiner's tip The probability of something not happening is 1– (the probability of it happening).

---

10 (a) Use of 19; $\frac{5}{19}$ (b) 0.75 **2 + 1**

Examiner's tip Notice that some of the information in the question is not used (the information about girls). To answer part (b), subtract the probability from 1 as wearing glasses and not wearing glasses are mutually exclusive.

---

11 (a) 0.8 **1**

(b) 0.6 **1**

(c) 0.4 + 0.2 = 0.6 **1 + 1**

(d) One card is both a 5 and a Club *or* not mutually exclusive **2**

Examiner's tip The answer to part (a) can be found from 1 – 0.2 or 0.4 + 0.1 + 0.3. Before answering part (c) you should check that the two outcomes 'It is a Club' and 'It is numbered 3' are mutually exclusive, that is, there is no card that is both a Club and a 3. The question makes this clear.

---

12 (a) 0·53 **1**

(b)

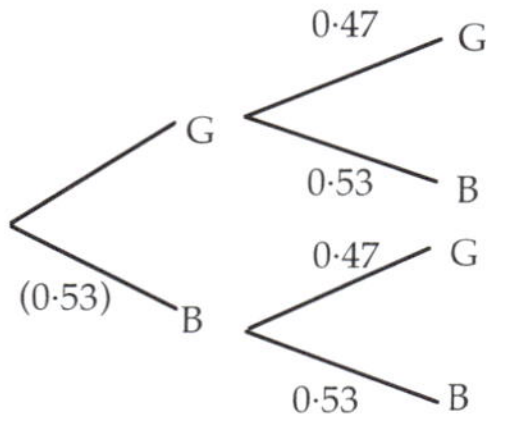

2

Question		Answer	Mark
(c)	(i)	BB	1
		0.53 x 0.53	1
		0.2809	1
	(ii)	GB or BG	1
		0·47 x 0·53 +0·53 x 0·47 = 0·4982	2

Examiner's tip You may assume that the two events (first child, second child) are independent and therefore multiply the probabilities.

5 MOCK EXAMINATION PAPER

Question			Answer	Mark
1	(a)		9 16, 22, 28	2
	(b)	(i)	19 (ii) $4 + 6 \times 9 = 58$	1+2
	(c)	(i)	+2 (ii) +6	1+1
	(d)	(i)	$2n - 1$ (ii) $6n - 2$	1+2

Examiner's tip Where there are 2 marks you will score 1 if you only make one error. Use the differences in part (c) to help you find the the *n*th terms in part (d).

Question			Answer	Mark
2	(a)		20 g	1
	(b)		375 g flour	1
			200 g cheese *and* 200 g butter *both correct*	1
			5 eggs *and* 25 ml mustard *both correct*	1
3	(a)		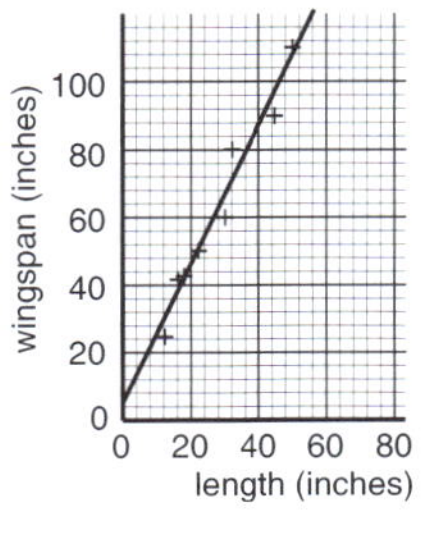	2
	(b)		positive (not strong)	1
	(c)	(i)	draw as above	1
		(ii)	about 30	1

Examiner's tip You can read the answer to part (c) (ii) from your line in part (i).

Question			Answer	Mark
4			110° – opposite angles of parallelogram	1
			40° – angle on straight line with 140°	1
			70° – exterior angle = 110°	
			r = 110°−q	1
			70° – parallel lines, FA, EB – corresponding angles	1
5	(a)		5.5 4	1+1
	(b)		means = 5.25, 4.2	1+1
			probabilities 0.525, 0.42	1
	(c)		Joyce – more experiments	1

Examiner's tip To find the probabilities in part (b) remember each result is the number of times out of 10.

Question			Answer	Mark
6	(a)	(i)	16	1
		(ii)	$2x - 6 = 5x$	1
			$x = -2$	1
		(iii)	$3x + 2 = 8 - 4x$	1
			$x = \frac{6}{7}$	1
		(iv)	$3x + 24 - 4x = 2x + 10 - 6x$	1
			$3x = -14$	1
			$x = -4\frac{2}{3}$	1
	(b)	(i)	$3x(x - 2y)$	1+1
		(ii)	$(x - 3)(x - 4)$	1+1
7	(a)		3 1 4 1 5 2 3 2 4 2 5 3 4 3 5 4 5	
			1 4 1 5 1 3 2 4 2 5 2 4 3 5 3 5 4	2
	(b)	(i)	$\frac{2}{20}$ or $\frac{1}{10}$	1
		(ii)	$\frac{6}{20}$ or $\frac{3}{10}$	1
		(iii)	0	1
		(iv)	$\frac{10}{20} = \frac{1}{2}$	1

Examiner's tip You can answer part (b)(iv) without counting. The cards cannot be the same, so one must be greater than the other. All the results for Sam are repeated for Ajit

Question			Answer	Mark
8	(a)		$2x(-2)^2 - 2a - 6 = 0$	
			$8 - 2a - 6 = 0$	1
			$a = 1\cdot$	1
	(b)		$2x^2 + x - 6 = (2x - 3)(x + 2)$	1
			other solution $x = 1\frac{1}{2}$	1

Question		Answer	Mark
9	(a)	0·33156......	2
	(b)	$\frac{30 \times 0.1}{\sqrt{64}} \approx 0.3$, (or 0.4)	1+1
	(c)	27.55, 27·65	1+1

Examiner's tip In part (b), choose approximations that will make the result easy to work out.

Question		Answer	Mark
10		Semicircle AB = $\frac{1}{2} \times 80 \times \pi \times 125.66$	1+1
		Radii $3 \times 40 = 120$	1
		Rectangle ABCD = 400	1
		$PS^2 = 40^2 + 60^2 = 5200$	1+1
		PS = 72·11	1
		Total=$125.66 + 120 + 400 \times 72.11 = 934$	1

Examiner's tip This question expects you to decide for yourself how to tackle it. Don't forget that you will not always be told when to use Pythagoras.

Question		Answer	Mark
11	(a)	$(4000 - 1500) \times \frac{40}{13} = 7692$	1+1
	(b)	10×1000	1
		$\times$ 0.313 3130	1+1

Examiner's tip If in doubt about which way to use the ratio look back at the definition – vertical : horizontal = 13 : 40 – so the horizontal distance will be greater than the vertical.

Question		Answer	Mark
12	(a)	using mid-points 45, 55, etc.	1
		(45x2 + 55x16 etc) ÷ 100	1
		69	1
	(b) (i)	18, 59, 86, 96, 99, 100	1
	(ii)	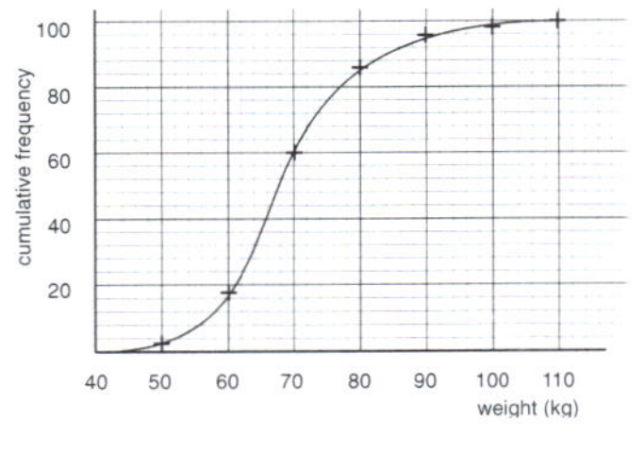	2
	(iii)	median = 68 kg	1
		interquartile range = 75 − 62 = 13	1

Examiner's tip Don't forget to plot the points at the right hand ends of the intervals.

Question		Answer	Mark
13		3.7 ÷ 2.54	1
		$\times$ 500 000 ÷ 63360	1
		= 11.495... = 11.5 miles	1

Examiner's tip You will lose a mark if you do not round the answer.

Question	Answer	Mark
14	Line parallel to AB 2cm away	**1**
	Arc of circle centre P radius 5 cm	**1**
	Line bisecting angle DCB (45°)	**1**
	Part of line indicated	**1**

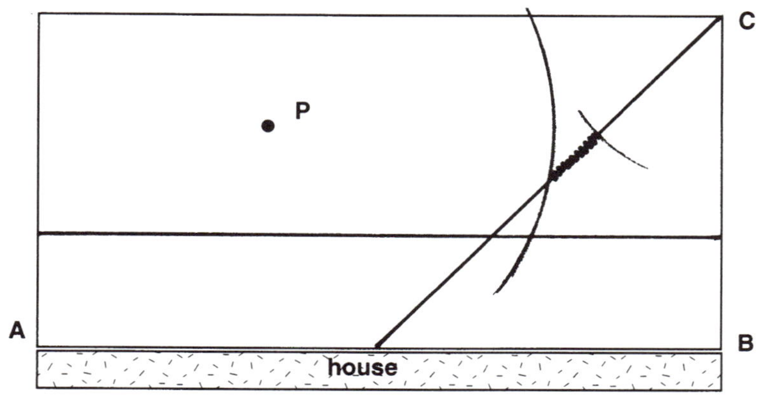

Examiner's tip Don't obscure your construction lines when you show where the drier can go. Remember – you often need compasses and a protractor (angle measurer)

Question	Answer	Mark
15 (a)	$\dfrac{10 \times 20 + 256}{3} = 152$	**1+1**
(b)	$3h = 10f + 256$	**1**
	$10f = 3h - 256$	**1**
	$f = \frac{3h - 256}{10}$	**1**
(c)	29.3	**1**
(d)	No – if $3h < 256$, i.e. $h < 256 \div 3 = 85$, then arm length is negative.	**1**
16 (a)	$74 \times \tan 37° = 55.8$	**1+1**
(b)	sin(angle KBC) =	**2**
	angle KBC= 25.4°	**1**
(c)	$BC^2 = 130^2 - 55.8^2 = 13790$	**1**
	BC = 117.4	**1**
	AB = 191.4	**1**

Examiner's tip You may score a mark in part (b) if you show you are using sine, even if you make a mistake. In part (c), you could use $130 \times \cos 25.4$ to find BC.